FROM BOSTON TO THE BERKSHIRES

A PICTORIAL REVIEW OF ELECTRIC TRANSPORTATION IN MASSACHUSETTS

STEPHEN P. CARLSON

with

THOMAS W. HARDING

BULLETIN NUMBER TWENTY-ONE

BOSTON, MASSACHUSETTS

BOSTON STREET RAILWAY ASSOCIATION, INC.

1990

First Edition

Published by the

BOSTON STREET RAILWAY ASSOCIATION, INC.

Post Office Box 181037
Boston, Massachusetts 02118-1037

Printed in the United States of America

Front Cover Photo: Type 5 lightweight of the Boston Elevated Railway no. 5734 waits at the Canal St. (North Station) terminal of the Green Line in Boston on July 15, 1979, during its first trip over the entire system since its return to the Hub after two decades of retirement at the Seashore Trolley Museum in Kennebunkport, Maine.   *Stephen P. Carlson*

Back Cover Photos: (Top) Because of wartime gasoline rationing, Union Street Railway "Electromobile" 602 has this New Bedford street to itself on August 22, 1945. (Bottom) On Memorial Day a decade later "All-Electric" PCC car 3215 of Boston's Metropolitan Transit Authority lays over between runs at Arlington Heights.   Top: *Lawson K. Hill*; bottom: *Russell E. Jackson*

Library of Congress Cataloging-in-Publication Data

Carlson, Stephen P., 1948-
　　From Boston to the Berkshires : a pictorial review of electric trans-
portation in Massachusetts / Stephen P. Carlson with Thomas W.
Harding. — 1st ed. — Boston, Mass. : Boston Street Railway Associ-
ation, 1990.
　　　　　p.　　cm. — (Bulletin / Boston Street Railway Association ; no. 21)
　　Bibliography: p. 159-160.
　　ISBN 0-938315-03-X

　　1. Street-railroads—Massachusetts. I. Harding, Thomas W., 1924-　　. II. Title.
III. Series: Bulletin (Boston Street Railway Association) ; no. 21.
TF724.M4C37 1990　　　　388.4'6'09744—dc19　　　　87-5124
　　　　　　　　　　　　　　　　　　AACR2　MARC CIP 9/89

Library of Congress

CONTENTS

Several of the individuals whose work appears in this book are seen in this group portrait from a June 16, 1940, railfan excursion on the Union Street Railway in New Bedford. Among those who can be identified are Horton Banks (second from left), Bill Maier (with hand on trolley rope), Robert Gerstley (in dark jacket in front of door), Bill Riccitelli (with uniform cap next to Gerstley), Linc Harrison (in second row to right of door), Dick Wonson (to right of Harrison), Charles Duncan (in light suit with camera case), Tom Brown (to right of Duncan), Fred Williams (in uniform cap and dark shirt), Stan Hauck (fifth to the right of Williams), and Ted Santarelli (third from right).

Note on Spelling:

Throughout this book, the old form "borough" has been used consistently in the spelling of town and company names, for, with the exception of the City of Attleboro, this spelling is that found in official records.

PREFACE

THIS VOLUME presents a pictorial review of street railway and other electric transit operations in the Commonwealth of Massachusetts. It is not intended as a history of such properties beyond the brief introductory sketches and the data presented in the captions. A vast wealth of such information has appeared in print, and the reader is referred to the items listed in the bibliography. One will not find rosters here, nor, except for a few contemporary items, are system maps included.

The focus here is on passenger operations, although a brief chapter covers trolley freight and express service. Outside of some converted passenger cars, non-revenue equipment is absent. The variety of such rolling stock is so great that it is deserving of a book of its own. Since this is a work on electric transit, trackless trolleys and the electrified operations of steam railroads are covered.

The allotment of space is roughly proportional to the relative size and importance of the property. No hard-and-fast formula was used, however; the number and quality of the available pictures was the determinant. Emphasis is placed on the period from 1920 until abandonment. Not only is there more material for that era, it is also within the memory of many readers.

This book is an outgrowth of a joint project by the authors to produce a pictorial history of public transportation in Worcester. In assembling data for that work, it became apparent that there has been no treatment of street railways on a statewide basis since Professor Edward S. Mason's economic history in 1932. This effort is an attempt to partially fill that gap.

The research for and writing of the text and captions, as well as the layout and design, has been the responsibility of Steve Carlson. Tom Harding did considerable work gathering photographs, and his input has played a major role in shaping the final product.

This album was assembled from the work of many photographers, and each photograph has been credited to its creator wherever possible. This has not always proven to be an easy task, for railfans have always conducted a trade in pictures, often, unfortunately, not noting the original source. Thus, errors in attribution may be present, and we wish to express our sincere apologies. Where appropriate, we have added the name of the collection from which the print used has come. Two major exceptions should be mentioned. Since the late Charles A. Duncan's collection of negatives is intact, all views that he took (or had copy negatives for) are credited solely to him regardless of the source of the particular print used. Similarly, official Boston Elevated Railway photographs are only attributed to the company. The authors owe a great debt to the late Richard L.

Wonson and others for preserving these historic resources and making them available for use here.

To single out individuals for their contributions to this project would only serve to slight those of others. Thus, we wish to thank the following persons for making available photographs, furnishing information, providing encouragement, reviewing text and captions for accuracy, or otherwise assisting us in this endeavor: Edward A. Anderson; Horton Banks; James F. Beaulac; Philip C. Becker; Philip Bergen; Laurence M. Blanke, Jr.; James D. Brock; Charles A. Brown; Arsen Charles; Frank J. Cheney; George Chiasson; Norton D. (Skip) Clark; Bradley H. Clarke; Charles W. (Chuck) Crouse; O. R. Cummings; Gerald F. Cunningham; John P. Debo, Jr.; Kenneth F. DeCelle; Norman Down; Kevin T. Farrell; William T. Grimes; the late Stanley M. Hauck; Lawson K. Hill; Christine L. Lenihan; Daniel T. Lenihan; Frederick J. Maloney; Raymond G. McMurdo; Allen Morrison; Russell F. Munroe; Jim Nigzus, Jr.; Win Nowell; Foster M. Palmer; Richard Phillips; William Quance; John D. Rockwell, Jr.; Fred W. Schneider, III; Burton B. Shaw; C. L. Siebert; E.A. Silloway; Richard W. Symmes; Anthony F. Tieuli; and Roger G. Tobin.

Thanks must also be expressed to the dedicated group of individuals and the Beverly Historical Society for their fine efforts in preserving and making available the Walker Transportation Collection. Begun as the personal collection of the late Laurence Breed Walker, it has become unquestionably the finest source of New England transportation materials in any public repository.

To those who have assisted us but whose names we have forgotten, we must express our sincere thanks and apologies. Without the contributions of all of those named and unnamed this book would not have been possible. Last only because of tradition and certainly not least, we must acknowledge the strong and patient support offered during the course of compiling this volume by the two women in our lives: Mrs. Paul (Martha) Carlson and Virginia Harding.

Finally, it is to the pioneering street railway enthusiasts of New England such as Roger Borrup, Charles A. Duncan, Harold D. Forsyth, Theodore Santarelli de Brasch, Donald E. Shaw, Carl L. Smith, and William H. Watts, whose research and photography provided the basis for much of this book, that we gratefully dedicate these pages.

STEPHEN P. CARLSON
THOMAS W. HARDING

5

In 1902 the J. G. Brill Co. of Philadelphia delivered two dozen 14-bench open streetcars to the Old Colony Street Railway. Car 1597 of that lot is seen in Jackson Sq. in East Weymouth. Passing successively to the Bay State and Eastern Massachusetts Street Railways, the car was last used to transport passengers to the 1931 Brockton Fair and fell victim to the scrapper's torch in 1932. A half-century later, this group of cars served as the model for the 15-bench opens constructed for the Lowell National Historical Park.

INTRODUCTION

THE STREET RAILWAY IN MASSACHUSETTS

MASSACHUSETTS became the third state in the United States to have street railway service when, on March 26, 1856, the Union Railway Co. began running between Central Sq., Cambridge, and Bowdoin Sq., Boston. Other horsecar lines soon followed throughout the commonwealth, coming to Lynn in 1860, Worcester in 1863, Lowell in 1864, and Springfield in 1870. By the 1880s most of the state's major population centers had one or more lines.

But the horsecar had reached its limits, and the 1880s saw a search for substitute motive power. Although Boston briefly considered cable cars, the most promising alternative was electricity. That Massachusetts would be in the forefront of this movement was natural, for Lynn was home to the Thomson-Houston Co., a predecessor of General Electric and a pioneer in the development of electric traction. Indeed, the first trolley cars in the state ran from its plant on April 2, 1888.

The introduction of electric power brought about a boom in street railway construction which would last until about 1905. In 1890 only 157 out of 664 miles of railway used the new power. A decade later, less than 10 of 1,973 miles employed horsepower. Growth slowed after 1903, but mileage continued to rise until 1918, when it peaked at slightly over 3,000.

In the 1890s electric railways promised "a new epoch in American economic life," wrote Professor Edward S. Mason of Harvard in 1932. Streetcar lines "radiating like the spokes of a wheel from every center of population brought the country man into town and took the city man to the country." The "streetcar suburb" had been born.

Rival groups competed for coveted franchises. Promoters such as E. P. Shaw of Newburyport and his sons appeared to build lines, as much for their own profit as the benefit of the public. Promotion thrived because the public hungered for the cheap, readily-available transportation street railways promised and formed a "ready customer" for the stock issued by the promoters.

But promotion was not without its cost. Not all schemes were sound; in the two decades after 1890 at least 18 railways were abandoned without ever having been built, often at a loss to their investors. Promoters, having little intention of holding lines on a long-term basis, were also more than willing to agree to local demands for concessions and services which would haunt railways in later years. As the *Springfield Republican* wrote of one promoter in 1899, the "promises fall as thick as raindrops in a storm." Furthermore, since they often awarded construction contracts to their own firms, they expanded their profits by minimizing expense. As F. J. McLeod of the Public Service Commission stated in 1917, "many of the roads were poorly and cheaply built."

This is not to say that all promoter-built lines were economically unsound and technically inadequate; many valuable miles came into existence through their efforts. Overall, they fulfilled a public need and helped build a railway network which gave Massachusetts "the most extensive mileage in proportion to area and population of any state in the Union" even as late as 1927.

As expansion occurred, the number of operating companies increased. Use of separate firms to build each route had distinct advantages for the promoter, but created some public inconvenience and often meant higher operating costs. Thus, a trend toward consolidation of smaller properties into larger entities developed, reaching its apex around 1911.

Consolidation took many forms, the most common of which involved the total merger of the properties involved. In other instances, one firm leased its physical plant to another, but kept its corporate existence. Finally, lines that were nominally independent were owned and managed in common. The voluntary trust, or holding company, was the usual means by which this last form of consolidation took place.

Although economies of scale were realized through such mergers, they often resulted in the combination of several financially precarious firms into a larger financially troubled corporation. Dividends were few and far between.

Operating costs rose sharply in the 1910s. The almost-universal nickel fare became inadequate to cover expenses, and the Public Service Commission was slow to grant fare increases. Unregulated jitney buses drew off the discretionary riders on which lines depended. "The result," wrote Professor Mason, "was that the small companies collapsed, the largest companies abandoned lines, and receivers appeared in the land."

The financial condition of the industry brought great concern to the men on Beacon Hill. The state's attitude was best stated by

One of the earliest streetcars in Massachusetts, Lynn & Boston Railroad Co. car 2 passes the Western Burial Grounds at Market Sq., West Lynn, on the opening day of the line, November 2, 1860. Horsecars dominated urban transit in the commonwealth until the early 1890s. The Lynn & Boston was one of the two companies around which later promoters built the state's largest street railway—the Bay State.

Carlson Collection

The newest streetcars in Massachusetts as of 1989 are the Type 7 cars built for the Massachusetts Bay Transportation Authority between 1986 and 1988. A two-car train waits at Brigham Circle between runs on the Huntington Ave. line in January 1989.

Carlson Collection

Governor Calvin Coolidge in 1919: "Transportation is a public necessity of the first importance.... If it cannot be paid for by the car rider, the expense must be met by . . . a contribution from the public treasury."

In 1918 and 1919 the General Court stepped in to rescue the state's two largest properties through the medium of public control and authorized cities and towns to subsidize losses on local routes or even to acquire and operate street railways themselves. Legislation also allowed railways to operate buses and gave the new Department of Public Utilities power to regulate bus service. That regulation usually benefitted existing railways by denying certificates to competitive bus lines.

But while receiverships declined in the 1920s, so did the streetcar mileage. The automobile had become a serious competitor. In 1920 there was one car for every twelve residents of the commonwealth; a decade later the ratio was one to four. Railway mileage dropped by half in that same period.

Although some lightly-patronized lines were not replaced, abandonment after 1920 usually meant the substitution of buses for streetcars rather than the total end of local public transit as it had before. Buses of the era were often small and uncomfortable, but they had lower capital and operating costs, required no fixed infrastructures, and could be readily shifted to meet changing transit needs. Most important, bus substitution was a means of reducing costs while maintaining service.

By the time the Great Depression struck in 1929 it was only a matter of time before most of the state's railways converted completely to buses. Only the Boston Elevated remained committed to the streetcar, and even it made major changes, expanding bus routes and introducing trackless trolleys.

As of 1940 only five companies still ran streetcars, and the Springfield Street Railway would be converted before year's end. World War II gave a temporary reprieve to trolley lines, but by mid-1948 all properties except Boston had junked them.

Boston would continue to operate streetcars, largely because of the presence of the streetcar subway into downtown. Indeed, in the early 1960s Boston looked at the possibility of eliminating all street-running routes and operating only within the subway and on two completely private rights-of-way. A decade later, as the anti-highway movement came into its own, attitudes had changed, and the overall future of the system, extensively upgraded in recent years with federal and state funds, seems secure. Today, except for a short tourist-oriented operation by the National Park Service in Lowell, Greater Boston is the only area of the commonwealth operating electric transit vehicles, and it will probably remain so for the foreseeable future.

STREET RAILWAYS OF MASSACHUSETTS – DECEMBER 31, 1916

Operating Company	Mileage		Passengers	Cars		
	Route	Track		Open	Closed	
Bay State	762.290	992.060	220,566,576	1,108	1,022	(1)
Berkshire	133.760	161.980	19,759,779	68	75	(2)
Blue Hill	19.730	19.990	1,829,837	14	7	
Boston Elevated	229.307	482.863	662,446,619	1,357	1,973	(3)
Boston & Worcester	48.920	83.620	13,144,104	23	53	
Bristol & Norfolk	6.573	6.696	272,724	6	3	
Brockton & Plymouth	22.480	24.840	1,937,429	15	11	
Concord, Maynard & Hudson	18.165	18.945	1,430,488	7	8	
Connecticut Valley	44.876	47.201	4,246,218	19	20	
Conway Electric	5.910	6.500	51,993	1	2	
East Taunton	11.248	11.424	1,060,260	4	4	
Fitchburg & Leominster	33.690	41.270	7,907,972	24	30	
Holyoke	58.323	72.309	14,746,292	75	68	
Interstate Consolidated	22.440	26.030	3,967,029	—	—	(4)
Linwood	2.230	2.280	610,880	—	6	
Lowell & Fitchburg	17.630	18.000	1,089,765	—	7	
Massachusetts Northeastern	120.420	128.450	15,501,169	81	45	(5)
Middlesex & Boston	105.801	130.323	19,519,893	149	113	
Milford, Attleborough & Woonsocket	28.490	29.720	1,964,248	14	9	
Milford & Uxbridge	53.858	56.677	5,316,230	26	34	
Nahant & Lynn	3.660	6.790	882,859	12	5	
New Bedford & Onset	36.990	44.050	2,350,121	17	11	
Norfolk & Bristol	20.470	22.032	1,758,708	10	11	
Northampton	24.360	27.490	5,099,475	26	21	
Northern Massachusetts	44.900	47.840	4,293,738	35	24	
Norton & Taunton	29.272	29.492	1,270,762	—	—	(6)
Norwood, Canton & Sharon	6.073	6.282	214,999	3	4	
Oak Bluffs	5.270	6.475	93,742	6	—	
Plymouth & Sandwich	17.080	17.430	83,783	3	2	(7)
Point Shirley	1.200	1.200	188,543	—	2	
Providence & Fall River	10.091	10.711	585,340	7	8	
Shelburne Falls & Colrain	6.950	7.430	217,550	2	2	
Springfield	141.490	187.880	50,663,990	150	249	
Taunton & Pawtucket	17.142	18.787	1,135,203	8	6	(8)
Union	42.120	64.060	25,190,806	90	107	
Ware & Brookfield	11.366	11.776	566,773	—	5	
Worcester Consolidated	250.560	300.080	72,706,030	132	297	
Worcester & Warren	19.607	20.098	781,649	4	7	

Source: *Fifth Annual Report of the Public Service Commission, January, 1918* (Boston: Wright & Potter Printing Co., 1918).

(1) Includes 34.790 route/40.070 track miles in New Hampshire and Rhode Island.
(2) Includes 26.950 route/28.220 track miles in Vermont.
(3) Excludes 13.974 route/37.447 track miles of rapid transit and 349 closed rapid transit cars.
(4) Operated with cars leased from the Rhode Island Co.
(5) Includes 42.380 route/45.960 track miles in New Hampshire.
(6) In receivership; only 18.870 route/19.492 track miles operated with 7 closed cars leased from Bay State Street Railway.
(7) Only 6.150 route/6.360 track miles operated.
(8) Receivers of Bristol County Street Railway reported 17.858 route/19.503 track miles.

The Massachusetts Bay Transportation Authority is the only operator of electric transit vehicles in the state in the 1980s. In March 1977 LRV 3428 loads at Reservoir station on the Riverside line. The LRVs were the first streetcars built in the United States in a quarter century. The line itself, converted to trolley operation from a steam railroad branch in 1959, has been an inspiration for the revival of light rail transit throughout the United States.

BOSTON

IN, OVER & UNDER THE HUB

BY LATE 1888 five of the six street railways operating in Boston—the Cambridge, the Metropolitan, the South Boston, the Boston Consolidated (an 1886 merger of the Middlesex and the Highland), and the West End—had been consolidated into the latter firm, creating the largest horsecar system in the United States. But it did not remain so for long, for one of the first priorities of the company was to find a replacement for equine motive power.

The story of President Henry M. Whitney's search for that solution, culminating in his visit to the pioneer electric trolley line in Richmond, Virginia, has become legendary. Suffice it to say that the first electric cars began operation on New Year's Day 1889 and that by Christmas 1900 the horsecar was no more.

But by that date the West End was no longer an operating company, having leased its property to the Boston Elevated Railway three years earlier. The Elevated had been chartered in 1894 to construct rapid transit lines across the city, the first of which—from Sullivan Sq., Charlestown, to Dudley St., Roxbury—opened on June 10, 1901.

The history of electric transportation in the city is inseparably linked to efforts to relieve the traffic congestion in the narrow, winding streets of downtown Boston. In 1892 a state-appointed Rapid Transit Commission recommended the construction of two elevated lines and a subway for streetcars under Tremont St. and the Boston Common. Construction on the latter project began in March 1895, and on September 1, 1897, the first subway in the United States opened.

The initial Main Line Elevated made use of this subway until 1908, when a separate tunnel under Washington St. was completed. In that same period an elevated line along Atlantic Ave. and a streetcar tunnel under Boston Harbor linking Boston and East Boston were completed. In 1909 the elevated reached south to Forest Hills. The year 1912 saw the Cambridge Subway opened between Harvard Sq. and Park St.; by 1918 that route had been continued to Andrew Sq., Dorchester. In 1914 the Boylston St. Subway was finished, and two years later the East Boston Tunnel was extended to Bowdoin Sq. As these rapid transit lines went into service, streetcar routes were adjusted to serve as feeders to the system.

But while physical growth was spectacular, the financial picture was far from bright. To save the system, the state assumed management of the property under the Public Control Act of 1918; in return for surrendering control, investors were guaranteed an annual return on their holdings. This arrangement would continue until 1947, when the commonwealth purchased the property and created the Metropolitan Transit Authority (MTA) to operate it.

Growth slowed between 1918 and 1947, but some expansion did occur. In 1919 the first leg of an authorized extension to Malden reached Everett Station. In 1924 the East Boston Tunnel was changed to rapid transit operation, and between 1927 and 1929 the Shawmut and Milton Branches of the New Haven Railroad became the Dorchester Subway and the Mattapan–Ashmont High Speed Trolley Line. On the streetcar system, the Kenmore extension opened in 1932 and the Huntington Ave. Subway in 1941.

The bus first appeared on the property in 1922, but, under the capable leadership of Edward Dana, general manager from 1919 to 1959, the system remained committed to electric-powered surface transit. Between 1936 and 1952 conversions to trackless trolleys outnumbered those to buses. By September 1958 all car lines except for those feeding the subway (Watertown, Boston College, Cleveland Circle, Arborway, Lenox St.) and the High Speed Line had been changed to buses or trackless trolleys. But the rubber-tired electrics were living on borrowed time. By April 1963 what had been the fifth-largest trackless network in the country had been reduced to the few lines using the Harvard Sq. tunnel.

Major rail transit developments under the MTA were the Revere Extension opened in stages between 1952 and 1954 and the Riverside line of 1959. Five years later the MTA was replaced by the Massachusetts Bay Transportation Authority. Encompassing a wider area than its predecessor, the MBTA has constructed the South Shore Line to Quincy and Braintree, replaced the Charlestown and Roxbury elevateds, and modernized the equipment and facilities of all its electrically-powered routes. While the Watertown line closed "temporarily" in 1969, and the future of the Arborway service was uncertain in 1989, it is clear that the streetcar as well as the rapid transit train will have a place in the transit scene in "the Hub" for years to come.

The Metropolitan Railroad was the largest of the companies operating in Boston prior to the West End merger of 1888. Typical of its equipment was this 7-bench open car assigned to the Dorchester Ave. route.

The West End's early electric cars were virtually identical to the horsecars they replaced. Indeed, many of them were converted from one motive power to another. Car 558 was one of 145 horsecars lengthened from 16 to 20 feet in the process. In service in 1893, it became a salt car in 1916.

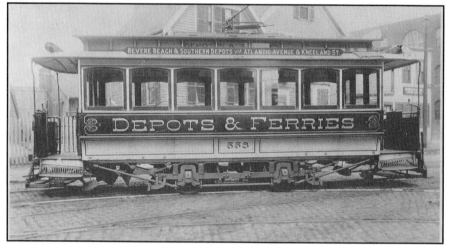

Seen on Dorchester St. in 1904, 7-bench open 2696 was one of 564 conversions from horse to electric power between 1889 and 1894. It was scrapped in 1915.

In the fall of 1891 the West End tested an experimental double-deck streetcar built by Pullman.

The largest single type of car on the Boston system was the 25-foot closed car, 1,202 of which were built or purchased from 1890 to 1900. Cutting its way through the slush on Cornhill at Washington St. in 1916 is car 810, a Newburyport product delivered in January 1892. The distinctive three-window vestibules, forerunner of the so-called "Boston front," were added to the cars after 1901 to comply with a 1900 law intended to protect motormen from the elements in the winter.

Boston has the distinction of being the first city in the Western Hemisphere and the fourth in the world to build a subway line. While proper Bostonians may have been horrified at the idea of the line encroaching on the Public Garden, the portal blended into the Olmsted-designed landscape. Nine-bench open 1653 leads a parade of cars out of the subway shortly after its opening. The 765 9-bench opens were the backbone of summer service until 1918. When the Boylston St. Subway opened in 1914, the Public Garden incline was replaced by an adjacent one in Boylston St. itself.

GENERAL BANCROFT'S PRIVATE CARS

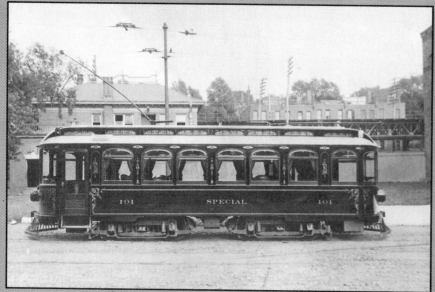

In 1904 the Boston Elevated purchased a private car for use by its president, General William A. Bancroft. Car 101, built by Kuhlman, was described as "one of the most perfectly appointed vehicles ever designed for use in the street railway service." After nearly 17 years as head of the Elevated, Bancroft resigned in 1916 and the car fell into disuse, although it was not disposed of until 1932.

Boston Elevated Railway

One of the most unusual parlor cars ever built for any railway in the country, single-truck parlor-plow 101 posed for its official portrait at Bartlett St. Shops in March 1900. Still carried on the service car roster in 1925, it represented a luxury not even the titans of mainline railroading could boast.

Boston Elevated Railway

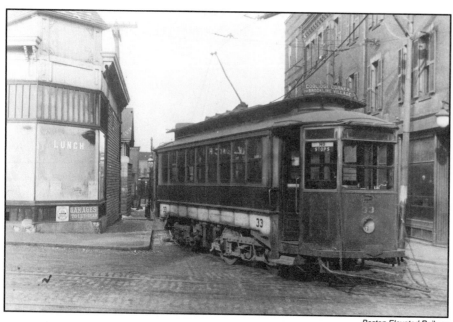

The first cars in Boston equipped with air brakes were the 60 closed cars with 26-foot bodies received in 1903 and 1904. They also introduced the "Boston front" used on most later cars through the 1920s. Car 33 was received from the Laconia Car Co. on November 17, 1903, and spent most of its life at the Allston carhouse, near where this picture was taken. Scrapping of the car was authorized on July 20, 1929.

Boston Elevated Railway

Many of the 25-foot cars were converted to work service after their passenger-carrying days were done. Test car 396, built by St. Louis Car in 1900, was one of the newest of its type. This view was taken in Chelsea Sq. in August 1938, 16 years before the car was sold to the Seashore Trolley Museum.

Charles A. Duncan

"SNAKE CARS"

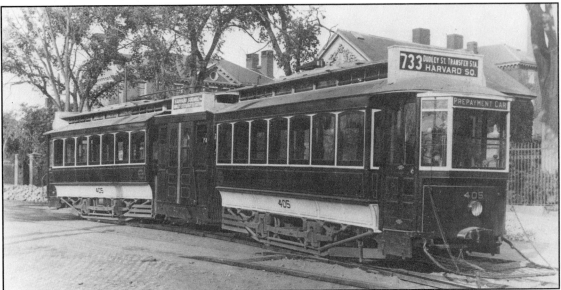

Boston Elevated Railway

In order to make better use of large numbers of small capacity closed cars and reduce manpower requirements, the Elevated combined pairs of them with new center sections to produce articulated cars. The first such vehicle was 405 (later 4000), completed in 1912. The articulateds, known as "snake cars" or "two rooms and a bath," provided needed capacity until new center-entrance cars could be acquired.

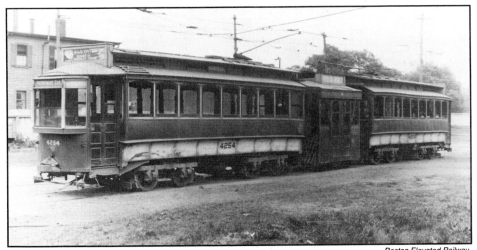

After building 69 articulated cars from 20-foot units, the railway proceeded to construct 122 more using 25-foot cars. No. 4254 combined cars 1390 and 1418, which had been built in 1896 by St. Louis and Laconia, respectively. This vehicle went to the scrapyard in 1921, three years before the last articulated was withdrawn from service.

Boston Elevated Railway

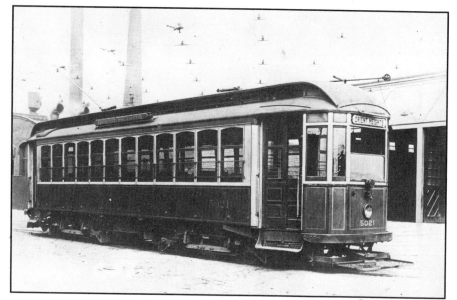

In 1905 the Boston Elevated bought 40 semi-convertible cars from Brill. Identified as Type 1 cars, they had 32-foot bodies and multiple-unit control, although only a few ever ran in trains. Car 5021 was assigned to the Eagle St. carhouse in East Boston, where this view was taken in May 1906.

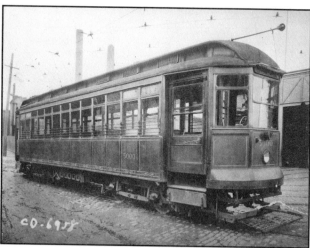

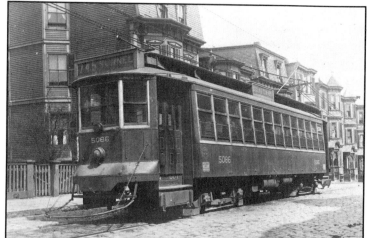

Even as the Type 1 cars were being ordered, BERy's shops were constructing an experimental semi-convertible car to the "Easy Access" design by John Lindall of its staff. Car 5000 (LEFT) was assigned to the East Boston Tunnel together with the Type 1s, and proved superior to the Brill design. Thus, in February 1906 the railway ordered 50 Type 2 units based on its design. Seen in East Boston in the late 1910s, car 5086 (RIGHT) has been modified by the addition of Hunter sign boxes on the roof.

Car 5071 was one of three Type 2s converted to compressor cars. The spring of 1950 saw it employed in the construction of the Revere Extension of the East Boston rapid transit line along with Differential dump cars 3618 and 3624. In 1972 car 5071 was sold to the Seashore Trolley Museum, while 3618 went to the Arden (Pa.) Trolley Museum two years later.

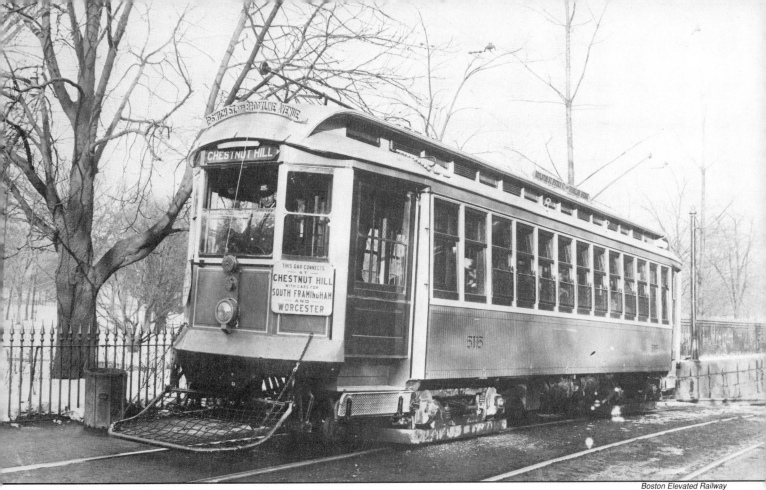

Type 3 semi-convertible 5115 (ABOVE) emerges from the Public Garden subway portal two days after entering service in December 1907. The 100 cars were nearly identical to the Type 2 units. While they were retired from passenger service by 1931, some 40 cars were converted to snow plows, several of which survive in 1988. Plow 5166 (RIGHT) works its way along Huntington Ave. at Copley Sq. on the day after the St. Valentine's Day blizzard of 1940.

Four Type 3s were converted into sand and salt cars. No. 5097 operates on Alford St., Charlestown, at Sullivan Sq. in October 1938. Although no longer manufacturing candy, the Schrafft's chocolate factory in the background remains a local landmark.

Between 1911 and 1914 four carbuilders delivered 275 Type 4 cars. They were the system's first all-steel surface cars. In June 1911 company employees demonstrated the operation of the prepayment system for the photographer.

The roof-mounted signs on the first 50 cars were later replaced by roll-signs above the front window. "Low sign" car 5235 is seen at Boylston and Arlington Sts. headed outbound in May 1933.

A total of 225 center-entrance trailers arrived between 1915 and 1918. The Type 4s received Tomlinson couplers to allow them to tow those units. Most of the trailers were retired by the mid-1930s, but a dozen lasted until 1944. Kuhlman-built unit 7194 was photographed shortly after being placed in service on April 4, 1919.

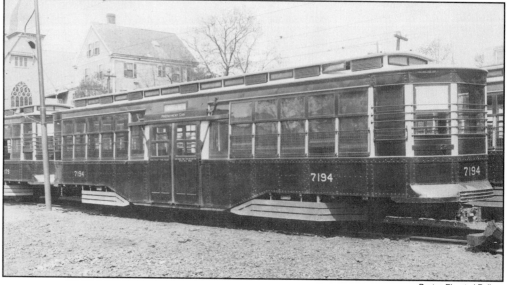

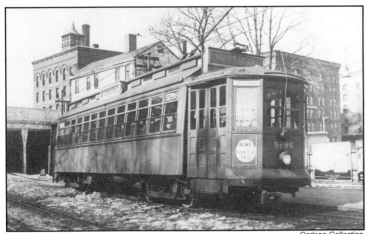

The High Speed Trolley Line between Mattapan and Ashmont represented the first conversion of a steam railroad branch for streetcar (light rail) operation, preceding the better-known Riverside line by 30 years. For two decades, Type 4s ruled this route. Laconia-built 5285 waits at Mattapan in the early days of 1940. The front sign boxes on all orders after the first were located at the ends of the roof monitor.

The Jewett Car Co. of Newark, Ohio, built 100 Type 4s. Car 5442 shares the venerable Summer St. bridge with bus 14 in May 1938.

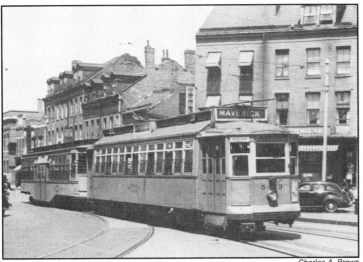

A year later 5423 hauls Brill-built trailer 7002 through Maverick Sq., East Boston. The Maverick–Suffolk Downs Race Track route was the last to use trailers.

Car 5209 on Gladstone St. in East Boston in 1949 wears the MTA map decal. While some of the Type 4s survived into the early 1950s, this car would be scrapped by year's end.

Two products of New Hampshire's Laconia Car Co. pose at the Seaver St. loop in 1948. Type 4 no. 5230 was built in 1911, while Type 5 no. 5696 carried a 1923 construction date.

In 1916 the Elevated ordered 100 center-entrance motor cars, followed a year later by 200 additional units. Two-thirds of the initial lot, including 6038 (RIGHT), were assigned to service through the East Boston Tunnel. Note the truck guards which were removed in 1920 and 1921. With the delivery of the second group, three-car trains such as 6225, 6232, and 6223 (ABOVE) became common sights on Beacon St. at Coolidge Corner, Brookline, for three decades. The temporary paper signs date this picture to the fall of 1919.

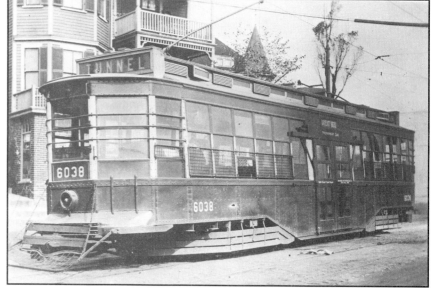

In 1921 the railway received a final group of 105 cars which were not equipped for multiple-unit operation. One of 75 units constructed by Kuhlman, no. 6392 leaves the Boylston St. subway portal in 1935. Note the front-mounted trolley poles, a distinctive feature of the center-entrance cars. The trolley rope passed through the roof at the center of the unit, where the conductor stood, a convenience in case of dewirements in the subway.

The New Haven Railroad's Roxbury Crossing station looms behind 6302 as the Laconia product makes its way toward Egleston Sq. in September 1938.

Arthur Fiedler was in the 10th of his 50 seasons as conductor of the Boston Pops Orchestra when Charles Duncan caught 6287 and 6283 turning from Massachusetts Ave. onto Huntington Ave. by Symphony Hall in June 1939. The unusual sight was the result of the use of the Huntington Ave. tracks for storing extra cars for the annual School-boy Day parade.

In 1930 center-entrance cars replaced Type 4s on the Watertown-Park St. subway route. In April 1936 a train consisting of 6029 and 6013 heads inbound at Newton Corner. Three years later Type 4s were reassigned to the line, and the center-entrance units were placed in storage. Rehabilitated for use during World War II, both 6029 and 6013 were scrapped in 1945.

On February 16, 1941, spectators line the still-unfinished portal of the new Huntington Ave. Subway at Opera Place (now Northeastern station) as the first train, carrying the official party, descends into the new tunnel. The $7.1 million project ended operation on the surface through Copley Sq. and eliminated the Boylston St. portal.

A train consisting of 6297 and 6271 is seen at Columbus Ave. and Centre St. in Jackson Sq., Roxbury, in March 1938.

The center-entrance cars could swallow great crowds in the subway. No. 6268 pauses for its portrait at the Brattle St. station during a May 1952 railfan excursion. The streetcar was scrapped in 1953, and the station itself virtually disappeared a decade later as the subway was altered to accommodate the construction of a new City Hall.

The solitary PCC car behind this train at the Arborway was an omen for things to come. In a little over a decade after this shot was exposed in October 1940, the streamliners would relegate the center-entrance units to the scrapyard.

Twenty-one center-entrance cars were converted to sand and salt cars between 1935 and 1945. In this capacity they ranged further over the system than they had as passenger vehicles. Car 6326 performs its duties on Dorchester Ave. at Park St. in Fields Corner in November 1938.

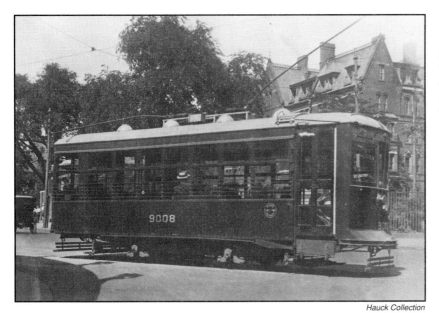

Like most major streetcar systems, Boston experimented with Birney cars but soon found them unsatisfactory. All but four of Boston's Birneys saw service elsewhere after their brief career in the Hub. One of 80 of the single-truck safety cars purchased in 1920, 9008 was sold in 1929 for export to Curitiba, Brazil.

Hauck Collection

BOSTON ELEVATED RAILWAY

FARE 10 CENTS

Horton Banks

In June 1936 the Boston Elevated purchased the Chelsea Division of the Eastern Massachusetts Street Railway. Included in the sale were facilities such as the Revere Beach terminal (ABOVE) and 49 semi-convertible and 10 lightweight streetcars. In June 1938 ex-EMSR 4341 and 4406 (ex-7028) (RIGHT) share that loop.

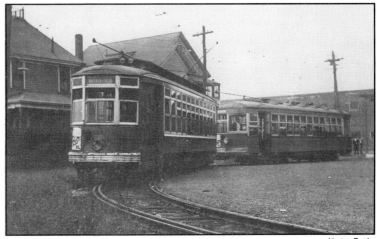

Horton Banks

The Boston Elevated acquired 471 Type 5 cars between 1922 and 1928 to replace old, obsolete equipment. One of 30 units received from Osgood Bradley in 1923, car 5766 was assigned to the Bennett St. carhouse in Cambridge. Bound for Harvard Sq., it loads on Massachusetts Ave. at Central Sq. in the late 1920s or early 1930s.

Carlson Collection

Donald E. Shaw

Charles A. Duncan

The Type 5s were distributed throughout the system. In June 1936 cars 5806 and 5862 (ABOVE) meet on Ferry St. at Malden Sq. Headed for Waverley Sq., Belmont, in early 1941, 5815 (ABOVE RIGHT) passes the Big Bear store, the area's first supermarket, on Mt. Auburn St., Cambridge. No. 5871 (RIGHT) is seen at Wilton St. and Brighton Ave. on the Allston–Dudley line in May 1938, less than four months before that route's conversion to buses. A decade later, 5560 (BELOW RIGHT), bound for Andrew station, operates on Columbia Road in Dorchester. In January 1939 car 5536 (BELOW) crosses the Warren Ave. bridge between Boston and Charlestown.

Charles A. Duncan

Horton Banks

Carlson Collection

Integration of surface and rapid transit service was a feature of the Boston system. Two of the many stations offering across-the-platform transfers between the two modes are pictured here. Car 5910 (ABOVE) enters the east loop at the Dudley St. station on the Main Line Elevated in July 1943. Already signed for an outbound trip, Brill-built 5865 (RIGHT) descends the incline into Maverick station in East Boston in May 1951.

Although transfers at South Station were slightly less convenient, riders of the Summer St. line from City Point had a wider variety to choose from in July 1938 (BELOW). They could take the Atlantic Ave. Elevated, the Cambridge–Dorchester Subway, or the local and long-distance trains of the New Haven and Boston & Albany Railroads.

The entire Type 5 fleet lasted long enough to have worn the map decal of the Metropolitan Transit Authority, although not all actually did so. Car 5740 pauses to load passengers at Roslindale Sq. on its way to the Charles River loop on September 28, 1951. On the following day trackless trolleys replaced streetcars on this route.

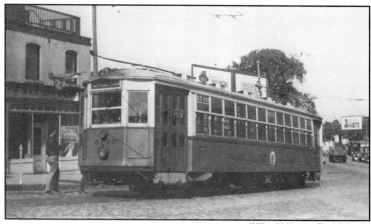

William V. Kenney, Tieuli Collection

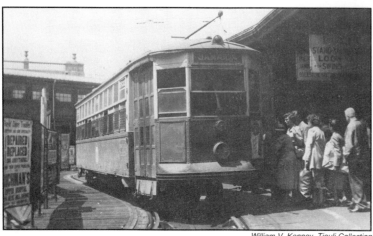

William V. Kenney, Tieuli Collection

In June 1949 the MTA converted the Jamaica–Dudley car line to bus operation. On the last day of rail service Laconia-built 5832 loads at the west loop of Dudley station.

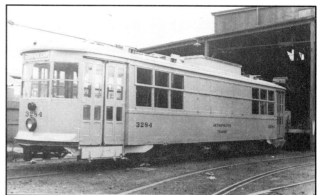

Stanley M. Hauck

The final Type 5 was converted into a line car in 1952 for use in the subway. The former 5970 is seen shortly after completion at the North Point carhouse in South Boston. Note the Tomlinson couplers, added to allow it to tow or be towed by PCC cars.

Four of the last nine Type 5s retired in 1959 were preserved at museums. In 1979 the MBTA leased 5734 from the Seashore Trolley Museum, and it has been available for charter service in Boston since that time. On its initial trip upon its return from Maine on June 27, 1979, it posed at Blandford St. with LRV 3463. Standing in front of the LRV are MBTA Instructor Dick Toomey, operator of the car, and MBTA supervisors Ted Butner and John Flaherty.

Stephen P. Carlson

The first known railfan excursion on the Boston Elevated occurred on June 19, 1938, when Charles A. Brown chartered the company's first PCC car for an all-day journey at a cost of $50. One of the many photo stops was the safety island on Bunker Hill at Elm St., Charlestown, outbound on the line from Scollay Sq. to Sullivan Sq. Car 3001 had been on the property just about a year at the time.

Gerald F. Cunningham

Boston Elevated Railway

In the fall of 1940 BERy began construction of a mockup of a PCC car having a modified windshield design, featuring a 20-degree rather than a 12-degree slope. The mockup, required because the Transit Research Corp., holder of the PCC patents, would not allow deviations from its standard specifications without it, is seen at Everett Shops in January 1941. By that time, fabrication of the 20 PCCs ordered in June 1940 was well underway, and they therefore came with the standard slope.

Boston's second order of PCCs was delivered early in 1941. Note the super-resilient wheels, blinker doors, non-multiple-unit couplers, and headlight wings on 3013 in this early view taken on Commonwealth Ave. at Boston University. By the time it was scrapped in 1971 it had received solid steel wheels, outward-folding doors, and multiple-unit equipment, while the wings had disappeared.

Carlson Collection

Between 1944 and 1946 the El received 225 multiple-unit PCCs from Pullman-Standard for the main trunk lines feeding the subway. One of those units, sporting the map decal of the new Metropolitan Transit Authority, rests at the back of the Reservoir carhouse yard around 1948.

In addition to the central subway, PCCs ran through the short tunnel at Harvard Sq., Cambridge. Note the left-hand door required on the cars because of station platform locations. This view of 3120 was exposed on September 5, 1958, the last day of streetcar service in Cambridge.

PCC 3061 passes the House of the Good Shepherd, a Catholic charitable institution, on Huntington Ave. at Parker Hill St. as it heads for North Station from the Heath St. loop in July 1959. Note the roof monitor, a feature added to 150 of the "Wartime" PCCs between 1948 and 1950.

In the early 1970s the MBTA began to paint vehicles according to the color codes used for its rail lines since 1965. Two cars in the green-white-and-gray livery adopted for the Green Line pass at the Beacon St. portal on a November day in 1976.

Paul R. Carlson

Chuck Crouse

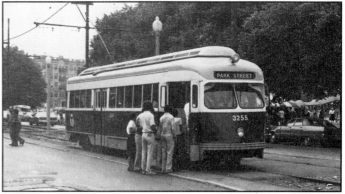

Stephen P. Carlson

Questions as to the reliability of the new generation of Boston streetcars led the MBTA to rebuild some of the PCC fleet. Car 3255 is shown (LEFT) on the production line at the Riverside shops in July 1977. A year later (ABOVE) it was back in service on Huntington Ave., loading passengers opposite the Museum of Fine Arts.

The survival of streetcars in Boston is the direct result of the presence of the subway. In January 1977 a two-car train headed by 3128 loads at Copley station for Beacon St.

Stephen P. Carlson

Foster M. Palmer

Because Superintendent of Rolling Stock & Shops Ralston B. Smythe disliked all-electric control, Boston acquired but one small group of PCCs without air brakes—and those units had been changed from "Wartime" cars as a favor to Pullman-Standard to allow it to gain experience producing the 1945 Model PCC within the limits of World War II production controls. Most of the 25 "All-Electrics" were initially assigned to the North Point carhouse in South Boston. Car 3203, headed for the Dudley St. elevated terminal, turns from West Broadway onto Dorchester St. in July 1953, five months before the end of rail service in "Southie."

Car 3204 at Heath St. loop in August 1977 exhibits the left-hand doors with which all but one of Boston's single-end PCCs were equipped. This unit was one of three sold to the Trolley Museum of New York in 1978.

Stephen P. Carlson

In 1951 Pullman-Standard delivered 50 "Picture Window" PCCs to the MTA, Boston's last new streetcars for a quarter century. Because of control differences from earlier streamliners, they were never trained with other PCCs. In the summer of 1974 cars 3292 and 3306 make the turn from Beacon St. onto Chestnut Hill Ave. at the end of the Cleveland Circle line.

In November 1983 "Picture Window" car 3279 heads a train outbound on South Huntington Ave. The E *Arborway* line was the last subway route to be operated with PCC cars. The wings around the headlight were applied to rebuilt "Wartime" and reconditioned "Picture Window" PCCs in the early 1980s.

Like their conventional predecessors, PCCs have supplied Boston with work cars. Fresh from the Watertown shops in 1977, "Picture Window" 3285 has been converted into a line car.

In June 1945 the Dallas (Tex.) Railway & Terminal Co. received 25 double-end PCCs from, Pullman-Standard. Car 623 is at St. Paul and Main Sts. downtown bound for the Oak Cliff section of the city in 1955, less than a year before streetcar service ended in "Big D." In 1958 and 1959 these cars were sold to the MTA, which needed double-end PCCs to retire the last Type 5s.

Maloney Collection

The major modification to the Dallas cars for Boston subway service was the addition of couplers, which required changes to the skirting and relocation of the anticlimber. Car 3327 (ex-Dallas 622) at the Broadway portal in February 1962 is on the shuttle instituted in November 1961 between this point and the Boylston St. subway station some 1,600 feet away. This remnant of the Tremont St. line lasted only until April 6, 1962.

Edward A. Anderson

Most of the Dallas cars were relegated to the isolated Mattapan–Ashmont High Speed Trolley Line. In later years they were converted to single-end, as attested by the absence of a headlight on the now-rear end of 3337 at Ashmont in 1977.

Stephen P. Carlson

By the late 1960s it became apparent that new cars would be needed in the near future. In 1970 the MBTA completed plans for its proposed Type 6 surface rail car, going as far as building a mockup of the front end of the car. At the insistence of the federal government, which would finance any new car purchases, Boston then joined San Francisco in the design of a United States Standard Light Rail Vehicle and the mockup was retired to the Seashore Trolley Museum.

Paul R. Carlson

Carlson Collection

The pilot LRV, seen outside the new Riverside carhouse shortly after arrival, was extensively tested in Boston between May 30 and August 14, 1975. Note the sandbags for load tests. The Boeing Vertol-built car subsequently became San Francisco Municipal Railway 1200, which accounts for the red-orange-and-white paint scheme.

Boston's first production LRV was 3415, which arrived on September 13, 1976, and entered service on December 30. Four days later the car loads on the outbound platform at Copley station.

Stephen P. Carlson

The 72-foot length and the articulation are readily apparent in this June 1977 view of LRV 3470 at Lechmere station.

Two generations of Boston streetcars sit between runs at Lechmere. PCCs and LRVs shared the Green Line rails until the end of 1985. Note rail car 1594 of 1904 vintage to the right of the LRV. The LRVs were the first Boston cars since the 1920s to display route designators.

The LRV fleet was plagued by mechanical problems, one of which involved the unreliability of the air-conditioning equipment. LRV 3455, unloading at North Station in May 1987, was one of 26 cars to receive Sutrak roof-mounted air-conditioning units during 1985 and 1986 in an effort to resolve this problem.

Of the 175 LRVs initially ordered, only 135 were delivered between 1976 and 1978. Because of continued problems with the sophisticated vehicles, the last 40 were cancelled in 1979. After 31 had been sold by Boeing Vertol to San Francisco, Boston repurchased the last 9 units in 1983. In September 1985 Muni 1301 (ex-MBTA 3567) heads a two-car morning rush-hour train inbound on Ulloa St. at West Portal in the "City by the Bay."

Stephen P. Carlson

In the spring of 1980 the MBTA borrowed three of Toronto's new CLRVs for revenue tests as part of the process of developing specifications for a Type 7 car. A two-car train consisting of 4027 and 4029 poses beside "Wartime" PCC 3250 at the Lake St. terminal of the Commonwealth Ave. line. Although the CLRV tests were successful, the Type 7 as ordered in 1983 resembled the LRVs already on the property with elements of the Type 6 and PCC thrown in.

Norton D. Clark

NO.7 軽量電車 | NO.7 SURFACE RAIL CAR

Stephen P. Carlson

The Type 7 entered revenue service during the summer of 1986. Built by the Japanese firm of Kinki Sharyo (with final assembly in Boston to meet federal "Buy American" rules), they had rounded rather than flat ends and reverted to traditional folding doors. These views of 3620 (ABOVE) and 3644 (RIGHT) were both taken at Fenway Park late in December 1986.

Stephen P. Carlson

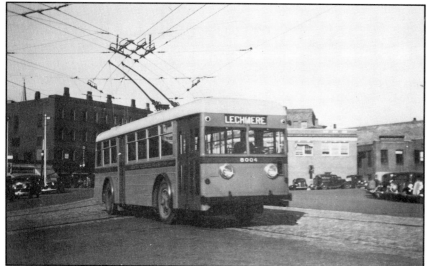

On April 11, 1936, the Boston Elevated inaugurated trackless trolley service on the Harvard–Lechmere route. Coach 8004, one of six purchased from Pullman-Standard for that operation, is at Mt. Auburn and Bennett Sts. near Harvard Sq.

Charles A. Duncan

In 1938 a group of 10 coaches with left-hand doors was purchased to allow the Huron Ave., Cambridge, service to be converted. Thirteen days after the commencement of trackless operation on April 2, 1938, coach 8122 is about to make the loop at the Aberdeen Ave. end of the route. These coaches remained in service until early 1959.

Carlson Collection

Boston Elevated Railway

Boston over the years purchased a total of 517 trolley coaches. Except for 5 prewar Twin Coach, 25 postwar ACF-Brill, and the current 50 Flyer units, all came from Pullman-Standard. Ten days after Pearl Harbor the Elevated signed a contract with that firm for 50 coaches. Because of wartime controls, the lot was reduced to 30 units, delivered in April and May 1943. Note the painted stanchions, a hallmark of wartime transit vehicles, and the war bonds symbol on the side of 8324 at Everett carhouse.

Anthony F. Tieuli

The first group of postwar coaches came in the spring of 1947, nearly three years after they had been ordered, a delay due to the tremendous backlog at the Worcester facility. The rollercoaster at Revere Beach can be seen behind coach 8340 as it waits at Wonderland station in 1959. The Pepsi bottlecap sign appeared on many trackless trolleys during this era.

Frederick J. Maloney

From 1950 until the end of the 1962 summer schedule the Everett Station–Revere Carhouse route extended beyond the carhouse to the Revere Beach Loop (later Wonderland station). In the last summer of operation, aluminum-bodied ACF-Brill coach 8717 is at Beach St. and Ocean Ave. A view of this same location decades earlier appears on page 47. Final abandonment of the Everett–Revere line, the last to serve the shorefront community, came on March 31, 1963, along with the entire Everett–Malden–Somerville services.

In 1951 the MTA received 90 trackless trolleys for the Arborway and East Boston conversions. Units 8483-8512 came with left-hand doors for Arborway service, while 8513-8542 received them in 1958 when they were shifted to Cambridge. These coaches served the remaining trackless lines in Cambridge until 1977. In February 1963 coaches 8517 and 8488 meet on Massachusetts Ave. just outside of Harvard Sq.

Richard L. Wonson

Stephen P. Carlson

The Harvard tunnel was the reason for the survival of the Cambridge trackless lines. In 1974 the MBTA ordered 50 coaches at a cost of $78,000 each to replace the 1951-vintage equipment on those routes. Shortly after entering service in the spring of 1976, Flyer 4002 leaves the tunnel to make the loop through the Bennett St. yard for its return trip to Huron Ave.

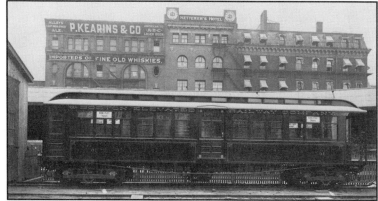

Boston's initial elevated cars resembled contemporary wooden railroad coaches with center doors. Wason-built 01 sits on the Canal St. test track in the spring of 1900. The elaborate lettering and striping were not repeated on production cars.

Boston Elevated Railway

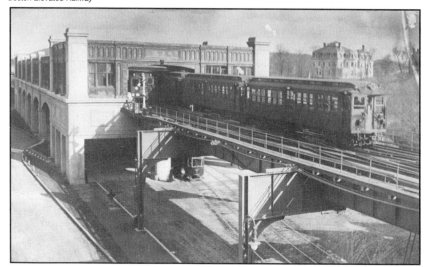

The Main Line Elevated opened between Sullivan Sq., Charlestown, and Dudley St., Roxbury, on June 10, 1901. Eight years later it reached south to Forest Hills. Four days before the November 22, 1909, opening of that extension two test trains of wooden cars sit at the new Forest Hills terminal.

Boston Elevated Railway

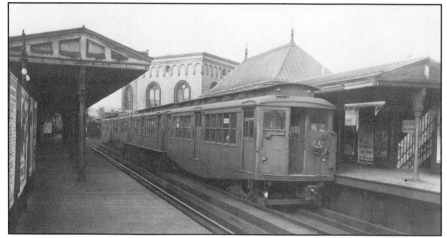

All-steel cars soon replaced wooden ones. This train, headed toward Everett at City Sq. station in Charlestown in October 1935, is made up of a mixture of deck-roof and monitor-roof units, including 0352, a 1921 Pressed Steel product. While the cars disappeared in the 1950s, and the station in 1975, the landmark Roughan Hall building in the background was restored in 1986.

Donald E. Shaw

All elevated rolling stock from the 1910s and '20s was replaced by the 01100s, built by Pullman-Standard in two lots in 1957 and 1958. They were the last rail transit vehicles built entirely in Massachusetts. In this scene from the early 1970s, a train leaves North Station, passing above the skylights and sign for the replacement underground station.

Stephen P. Carlson

The Atlantic Ave. Elevated served Boston's waterfront (LEFT) with stations at State St. (top) and Rowe's Wharf, and provided a link between the city's two major railroad terminals, North Station and South Station (ABOVE). The decline of the port in the 1920s and '30s was a major reason leading to the October 1, 1938, abandonment of this segment of the elevated system.

Between 1979 and 1981 the MBTA received 120 cars from Hawker Siddeley to completely reequip the Orange Line.

The New Orange Line

By the 1960s elevated railways had come to be viewed not as valuable transit links but as a cause of urban decay and blight. The Charlestown segment of the Elevated was replaced by the Haymarket–North extension to Malden in 1975, while the Washington St. end lasted a dozen more years before it was supplanted by the Southwest Corridor project. Boston's tallest structure, the 790-foot John Hancock Tower, forms a background for a southbound train at Massachusetts Ave. station in the first week of service on the new Orange Line.

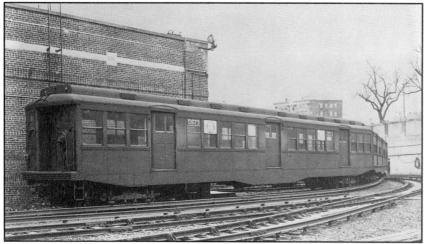

The Cambridge Subway cars were, at 69 feet, the longest transit cars in the world until surpassed by Toronto's H-1 class units in 1962. No. 0673 was part of a lot of 35 cars built by Pressed Steel in 1919. The MTA map decal dates this view at the Elliot Sq. shops to the late 1940s or early '50s.

The extension of the Cambridge–Dorchester Subway from Andrew Sq. to Ashmont in the 1920s used the right-of-way of the New Haven Railroad's Shawmut Branch. This conversion from railroad to transit use set a precedent for all future rapid transit construction in the Hub. Two trains meet near Savin Hill in the summer of 1939. The tracks to the right are the New Haven's Old Colony line, which would be used for the South Shore extension to Quincy and Braintree three decades later.

In 1963 the MTA acquired 92 modern cars from Pullman-Standard to replace all older units on the Cambridge–Dorchester route. A southbound train of 01400s loads at Park St., a major transfer point between this line and the streetcar subway.

The interiors of Boston's rapid transit cars have always been fairly spartan. High standee capacity was made possible through longitudinal seats and facilitated by the presence of a multitude of handholds and stanchions. By the time 01464 came in 1963, molded fiberglass had replaced wooden slats, although the change made little difference in passenger comfort.

A natural brushed aluminum finish was used on the cars purchased in 1969 for the South Shore extension. Car 01634 is seen at Eliot Sq. in May 1971. One aspect of the mid-1980s' rehabilitation project for these Red Line cars involved their being repainted in the standard red-and-white paint scheme.

Richard L. Wonson

Stephen P. Carlson

In 1924 the Elevated converted the East Boston Tunnel from streetcars to rapid transit. The vehicles purchased from Pullman for the line introduced the concept of "married pairs" of transit cars (i.e., units sharing some components) in order to reduce weight and keep within extremely tight clearances. Four units (ABOVE) can be seen in this view of the storage yard at Orient Heights in 1975.

The MTA purchased 40 PCC rapid transit cars for the extension of the East Boston Tunnel to Revere. In this December 1977 view, cars 0587 and 0548, the last and first of the group, are about to begin their inbound trip from Wonderland. Mismatching of pairs was common on Boston's rapid transit lines.

Stephen P. Carlson

In 1979 the MBTA began taking deliveries of new cars from Hawker Siddeley to replace all older cars on the Blue Line. In May of that year cars 0602 and 0603 pose behind Orient Heights shops.

Stephen P. Carlson

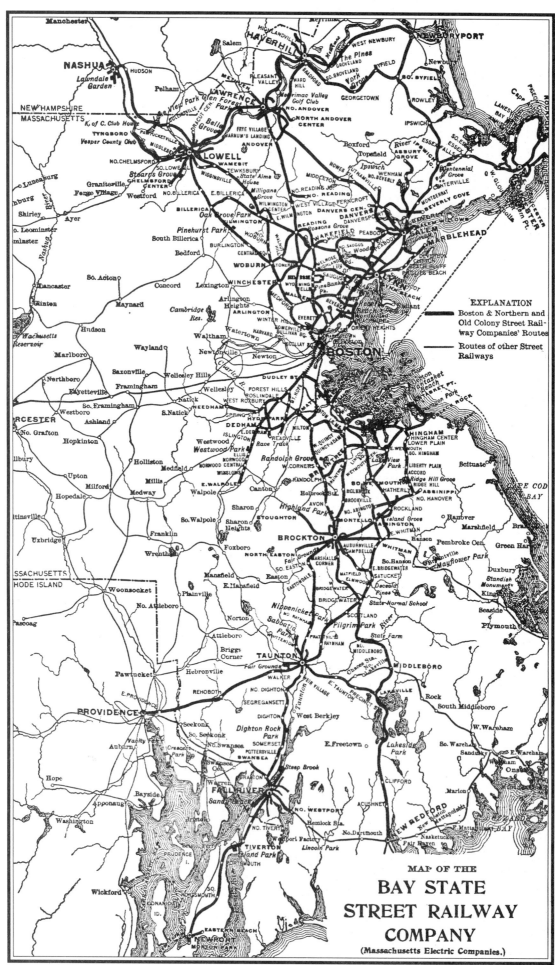

MAP OF THE

BAY STATE
STREET RAILWAY
COMPANY

(Massachusetts Electric Companies.)

EXPLANATION

Boston & Northern and
Old Colony Street Rail-
way Companies' Routes

Routes of other Street
Railways

FROM NEWPORT TO NASHUA

THE BAY STATE/EASTERN MASS. SYSTEM

THE BAY STATE STREET RAILWAY, with lines extending from Nashua, N.H., through Massachusetts to Providence and Newport, R.I., had in the 1910s the greatest mileage of any street railway in the world. It also had one of the most complex corporate histories. Chartered on April 6, 1859, as the Lynn & Boston Railroad, it became the Boston & Northern Street Railway in 1901 and the Bay State ten years later. Along the way, it absorbed 15 other companies, but, because of previous mergers, it came to include some 72 formerly independent properties.

While some of this merger activity occurred before 1899, most took place after that date as a result of the activities of the Massachusetts Electric Companies, a holding company formed by two Boston bankers. This trust purchased securities of 31 railways north and south of Boston, and then consolidated them into the Lynn & Boston or the Brockton Street Railway, which became the Boston & Northern and the Old Colony Street Railways, respectively, in 1901. The Old Colony became a part of the Boston & Northern on July 1, 1911, an event precipitating the name change to Bay State on August 8, 1911.

Most of the major cities served by the Bay State had horsecar service, including Lynn (1860), Salem (1863), Lowell (1864), Lawrence (1867), Taunton (1871), Haverhill (1877), Fall River (1880), Brockton (1881), Gloucester (1886), and Quincy (1888). The first electric operation occurred in Lynn in November 1888, and the majority of the predecessor companies were established as trolley lines in the ensuing decade.

The Boston & Northern and the Old Colony were managed as a single entity after 1901. The system reached 91 of the commonwealth's 351 cities and towns and also crossed the state line into New Hampshire and Rhode Island. (The Nashua and Newport properties were leased since a Massachusetts firm could not merge with out-of-state companies without special legislative permission from both states involved.) Entry into Boston came over the tracks of the Boston Elevated; the company never had a physical or operational link between the two parts of the property.

Hard hit by the economic crisis of the 1910s, the Bay State went into receivership in 1917. The state intervened to preserve the system, chartering the Eastern Massachusetts Street Railway in January 1919 to take over the assets of the Bay State. The Eastern Mass., which officially began operations on June 1, 1919, operated under the public control until 1949; by that time it was an all-bus system.

Abandonments had begun under the receiver, and by 1921 some 180 miles of track (out of a peak of 953 miles owned) had been discontinued. Included in these reductions were the Nashua and Newport operations, returned to their owners in 1918 and 1919, respectively, and the lengthy line from Bridgewater to New Bedford via Middleborough. The entire Gloucester division was abandoned on June 20, 1920, after the affected communities refused to pay the cost-of-service deficit for the lines, while the Hyde Park division trackage within the Boston city limits was leased to the Boston Elevated in 1923.

Contraction continued slowly in the 1920s. Buses were introduced in 1924, but until 1930 were a minor part of the picture. Conversions were spurred by the Depression, with the long intercity runs from Boston to Fall River, Lowell, and Lawrence being taken over by deluxe coaches in 1931. The Melrose division became all-bus in September 1931, followed in 1932 by Norwood and Taunton.

The practice of divisional conversions accelerated in 1935, as the Eastern Mass. abandoned the theory that the change "should await the wearing out of the railway plant." Now, it embraced the idea that conversion should depend only on the economics of purchasing the replacement buses. Lawrence went in June 1935 and Lowell in September. In 1936 Haverhill and Fall River followed, and the Chelsea division was sold to the Boston Elevated. Salem started off the 1937 program, followed by Lynn and finally Brockton. In less than seven years some 600 miles of trolley lines had been reduced to about 20. Only the Stoneham–Boston line and the Quincy division remained rail operated.

The Stoneham service quit in July 1946, but the last Quincy line hung on until May 1, 1948. The Eastern Mass. itself continued as a bus operator for two more decades, finally being purchased by the Massachusetts Bay Transportation Authority for $6.25 million on March 29, 1968.

Lynn & Boston horsecar 20 carries a full load of passengers as it proceeds outbound on Chelsea St. in Charlestown in 1874. Note the advertisement on the roof and the Marine guard at the gate to the Lower Officers' Houses (Quarters L-M-N-O) of the Boston Navy Yard.

The Stoneham Street Railway, organized in February 1860, became the East Middlesex in 1887. Its property was leased to the Lynn & Boston for 99 years in May 1893. East Middlesex 67 carries signs for the "Malden & Saugus" route in this circa-1890 view.

The oldest predecessor of the Bay State south of Boston was the Taunton Street Railway, which opened in September 1871. Horsecar 48 is at the Whittenton end of the Weir–Whittenton line in 1886.

Globe Street Railway 6 stands at North Main St. and Wilson Rd., Fall River, around 1880. The Globe became part of the Brockton Street Railway on January 19, 1901.

On November 19, 1888, the Lynn & Boston began operation of its first electric cars on the Highland Circuit line from Central Sq. to High Rock, Lynn. Motorman Emory G. Clark and Conductor Benjamin T. Moody pose with car 213 near the mid-point of this one-way loop. The route name theme is carried over into the plaid decoration on the vehicle.

The Lynn Belt Line Street Railway made its first complete circuit around the North Shore city on July 3, 1890. Riding on a three-axle radial truck, 12-bench open 17 is in front of the South Street Methodist Episcopal Church. The Belt Line was absorbed by the Lynn & Boston in October 1892.

Three cars meet at Reading Sq. around 1897. The two cars to the left were the property of the Reading & Lowell, while the unit to the right belonged to the Woburn & Reading. The Reading & Lowell and the Woburn & Reading were controlled by the same interests, and along with the Wakefield & Stoneham formed a route from Lowell to Lynn advertised under the slogan "From the Shuttle to the Shore."

Cars 9, 8, and 5 of the Manet Street Railway are seen at the company's Houghs Neck barn. The railway opened in 1890 and became part of the Quincy & Boston Street Railway in August 1893. Car 9, built by I. H. Randall of Boston in 1891, became Old Colony 3718 in 1901.

In the 1890s everyone wore hats, as this view of Hull Street Railway 8-bench open car 12 attests. The Hull and the Nantasket Electric Street Railway, which also served Nantasket Beach, became part of the Hingham Street Railway in 1898. A year later the Hingham was absorbed by the Hanover Street Railway, which shortly thereafter became the South Shore & Boston.

Carlson Collection

Hauck Collection

The names painted on early streetcars were generally destinations rather than the company name, as is exemplified by car 5 (ABOVE) of the Braintree Street Railway. Similarly, one of four 10-bench opens of the Haverhill, Georgetown & Danvers (RIGHT), seen crossing the Georgetown trestle, is lettered only "Haverhill & Georgetown."

Carlson Collection

The vast majority of cars owned by predecessor companies of the Bay State were of the single-truck variety. Among the exceptions were Georgetown, Rowley & Ipswich 12 (LEFT), a 13-bench open built by Newburyport in 1899, and Lynn & Boston 627 (RIGHT), a 25-foot closed car outshopped by Laconia in 1900. The open, loading at Governor Dummer Academy in Byfield, became Boston & Northern 1198 and survived until 1922.

William Dummer, Carlson Collection

Carlson Collection

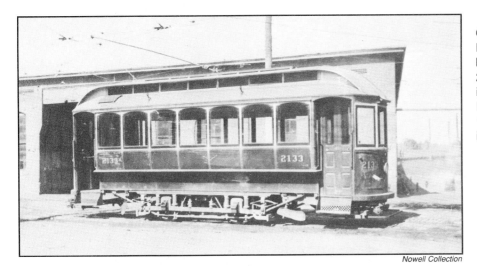

One of the first tasks of the combined Boston & Northern and Old Colony system was to renumber its rolling stock into a common roster. Car 2133 was a 20-foot unit built by Jackson & Sharp in 1893 as no. 2 of the Beverly & Danvers Street Railway. In this picture, taken in Lowell around 1920, a previous, more elaborate paint scheme is showing through on the front dasher.

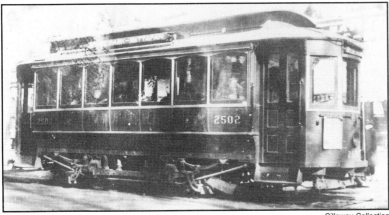

Supplied by Laconia in 1899 as part of the initial rolling stock of the Needham & Boston, this unit became West Roxbury & Roslindale 15 in November of that year. Seen at Mattapan Sq. as Old Colony 2502, it is on the Hyde Park–Mattapan via River St. line.

Parlor car 2697 (RIGHT) was one of two deluxe units taken over from predecessor companies. It had been built by Newburyport in 1898 as the "Lawrence" of the Newport & Fall River Street Railway.

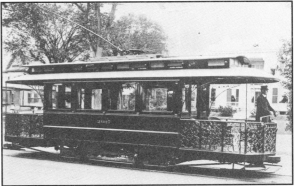

Headed for "Chelsea Sq. Only" from Beach St. and Ocean Ave., Revere, is 8-bench open 3394. Built in 1887 by Jones, it had been Lowell & Suburban 132 prior to the absorption of that company into the Lowell, Lawrence & Haverhill in November 1900 and the Lynn & Boston six months later. Movement of cars from their "home" properties was common.

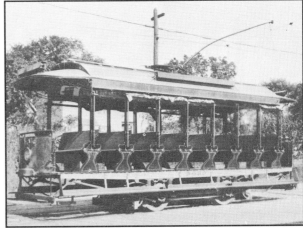

Eight-bench open 3469 was a product of the Ellis Car Co. of Amesbury. Long a part of that city's carriage industry, its career as builder of "The Best Car in the World for the Money" was cut short by an April 1894 fire which destroyed its factory.

In 1900 the West Roxbury & Roslindale purchased four 25-foot closed cars from Laconia, numbering them 112-115. In the consolidated roster they became Old Colony 502-505. The last of the group heads into the Westwood carhouse in Islington around 1906.

In 1900 the Lynn & Boston began a program to replace single-truck cars with double-truck units. No. 28, a 25-foot car seen on a run between Walnut and Myrtle Sts. and Eastern Ave. and Essex St., Lynn, was one of 55 such trolleys built that year in the company's Chelsea shops. They were among the few L&B cars that retained their original numbers throughout their lives.

Car 443 (LEFT) at Dummer Academy Junction in Byfield in 1910 was a 28-foot car rebuilt from Brill 20-foot units in 1897 by the Lowell, Lawrence & Haverhill's Lowell shops.

No. 632 at the Campello carhouse in Brockton was one of 25 closed cars with 30-foot bodies purchased for the Old Colony from Stephenson in 1902 as part of the rolling stock improvement program.

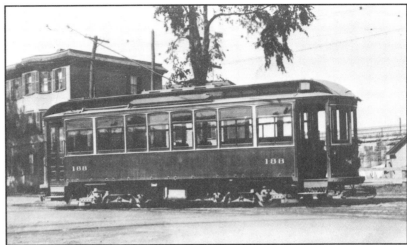

In addition to buying from commercial carbuilders, the Boston & Northern continued to lengthen single-truck cars and build new double-truck ones at Chelsea. Car 157 (LEFT) in Peabody Sq. in 1910 had been increased from 20 to 26 feet in 1902, while 188 at Lowell around 1920 (ABOVE) was part of a group of 25-foot cars outshopped in 1904.

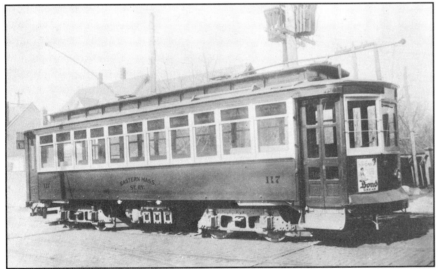

In 1921 and 1922 the Eastern Mass. rebuilt 40 double-truck closed cars for one-man operation. The most extensive conversion involved St. Louis Car-built 117 of 1902, shown here shortly after completion at Campello shops in Brockton in August 1921. As modified, the 30-foot unit closely resembled the system's 1300, 1700, and 4100-series semi-convertibles. It was scrapped in 1931.

The last double-truck closed car on the property was S-563, which spent its final years as a Root scraper and salt car at Fall River. Built in 1898 by the American Car Co., the 26-foot unit had originally been Providence & Taunton Street Railway car 46. This carhouse view was taken in February 1935, a year before its date with the junk dealer.

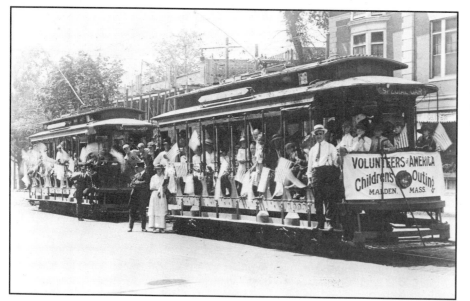

The Massachusetts Electric Companies' rolling stock program included double-truck open as well as closed cars. Boston & Northern 1003, part of a group of thirty 12-bench units acquired from Newburyport in 1902, is in Beverly on its way to Asbury Grove, the Methodist-run camp in Hamilton.

Duncan Collection

John Was Wise

IT didn't take him long to grasp modern improvements and appreciate the best of all up-to-date ways for a party to travel.

DON'T LET HIM HAVE ALL THE FUN

Try a special car. We can arrange to take you to any place connected by trolleys and bring you back at any time you wish, at a very reasonable cost.

Call, phone or write the office of the OLD COLONY STREET RY. CO., for rates and particulars when you have another trip in mind.

Division Superintendent.

Pilgrim John and his Pilgrim band
Came back to see this glorious land.
" Gadzooks," quoth he. " What can we see
" If we have to hoof it o'er the lea?
" We'll have to try, as I surmised,
" The SPECIAL CARS now advertised."
They hired a car, sped swiftly on.
" Forsooth, it's great," saith Pilgrim John.

Pilgrim John Series 1

Electric Railway Journal, Carlson Collection

The Boston & Northern and the Old Colony maintained an extensive promotional department to attract charter business to their cars. This mailing card was but one of a series of Pilgrim John materials issued in 1908.

Carlson Collection

Charter operations often took cars onto neighboring systems' rails to reach destinations such as Mayflower Grove on the Brockton & Plymouth Street Railway. Car 1571 was a 13-bench open built by Newburyport in 1899 as no. 100 of the New Bedford, Middleborough & Brockton.

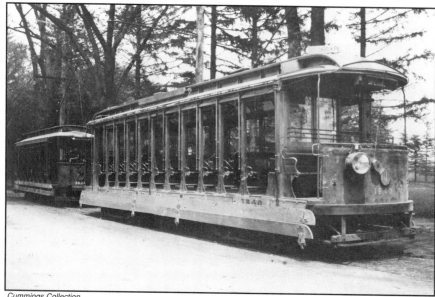

Bay State opens 1640 and 3624 are at Dighton Rock Park. The 14-bench unit was built by Stephenson in 1910 for the Old Colony, while 10-bench 3624 had been constructed by Brill in 1892 as Brockton Street Railway car 73.

Cummings Collection

In July 1914 the Boston Elevated Railway's photographer caught Bay State 14-bench open 1023 and Boston Elevated 971 on Salem St., Malden, during the reconstruction of the complicated junction of Salem, Ferry, and Main Sts. Both streetcars had been built by St. Louis Car, 1023 in 1902 and 971 in 1897.

To reduce costs, the Eastern Mass. ended regular open car operation in 1919. A group of 37 of the newest 14-bench cars on the property were sent to the Laconia Car Co. for rebuilding into closed cars. Car 1233 is seen in Lowell after reconstruction. Note the high steps which made the cars none-too-popular with passengers and resulted in their being confined to rush-hour service until scrapped in 1931 and 1932.

Rockwell Collection

Carlson Collection

A 1908 dash sign advertising the pleasures of riding open cars (LEFT) may have been carried by 14-bench unit 1620 in its early days, but had been long forgotten by the time it was photographed on Main St., Stoneham, in February 1940 in its reincarnation as snow sweeper B-620 (RIGHT). Ten Brill opens of 1902 were rebuilt for winter work service by the Eastern Mass. in 1922 and 1923.

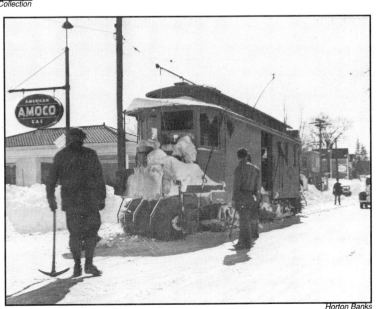

Horton Banks

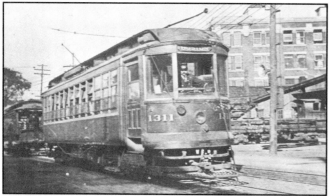

Walker Transportation Collection

The Boston & Northern's first semi-convertibles closely resembled the Type 2 and Type 3 cars of the Boston Elevated. Forty units came from J. G. Brill in 1906, and, at 46 feet overall, were the longest cars on the system. No. 1311 passes the General Electric Co. and the railway's West Lynn carhouse around 1914.

Stanley M. Hauck

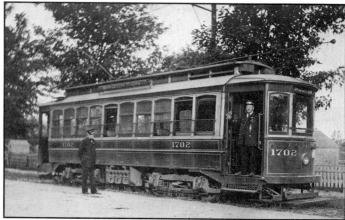

Rockwell Collection

In 1907 a total of 77 double-truck semi-convertibles were purchased from Kuhlman. Fifty cars were assigned to the Boston & Northern, numbered 1341-1390. The last survivor of the class was 1373 (LEFT), which ended its days as a service car at Quincy. To the right is double-truck shear plow P-188, a 1910 Wason product. The Old Colony's share of the order was numbered in the 1700 series. The crew of 1702 (RIGHT)—Lennie Sampson and Archie Savage—pose with their car on South Main St., Middleborough.

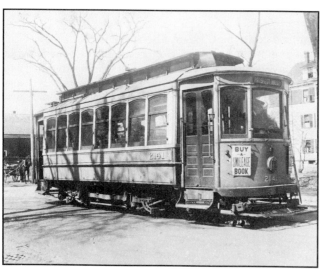

Carlson Collection

The 1907 order also included 10 single-truck semi-convertibles for the Boston & Northern. They were assigned primarily to the Melrose and Lawrence divisions. Car 2141 operates on Water St. in the latter city. Unsuitable for conversion to one-man service because they lacked air brakes, they were scrapped in the mid-1920s.

One of the earliest attempts to counter the trend toward heavier streetcars came in 1909 with the delivery of 44 semi-convertibles from Laconia. They averaged some 3 tons lighter than earlier units of the same general type. Cars 1401 and 1402 of that lot are lined up in front of the Reading carhouse.

Silloway Collection

The last opens purchased by the Bay State came from St. Louis Car in 1912. Eight were of the 12-bench variety, while 12, including 6103 at Lowell about 1920, had 14 benches.

In January 1917 the Bay State adapted about a dozen open cars for use conveying workers from Neponset to the Fore River Shipyard in Quincy. The conversions involved installing curtains with windows and heaters under the seats. The total cost of the conversion of the pilot car, shown here, was $247.10.

All but one of the 14-bench cars of the 6100 series were rebuilt to closed cars by Laconia in 1920. Eight of them, including 6111, were assigned to Lowell until scrapped in 1931. The Eastern Mass. logo on the car side appeared only on the rebuilt opens and the 5000-series Birneys.

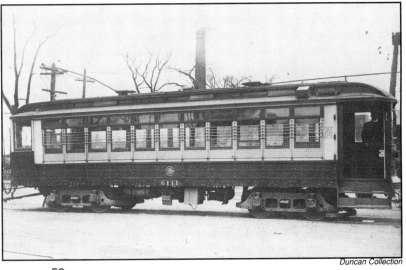

In 1912 the Bay State purchased 30 semi-convertibles from the St. Louis Car Co. Cars 4101 and 4102 spent their entire life in Fall River, being scrapped shortly after the end of rail operation in the Border City on September 20, 1936.

Hauck Collection

Charles A. Duncan

Horton Banks

A little more than two weeks before the end, 4129 is on Bedford at Third St., Fall River. With minor exceptions, the 4100s were identical with the 1391-1422 class semi-convertibles of 1909.

Car 4107 was last used as a newspaper car running between Haymarket Sq., Boston, and Lynn by way of Chelsea. Shown here at the West Lynn carhouse, it was withdrawn in 1934 and junked two years later.

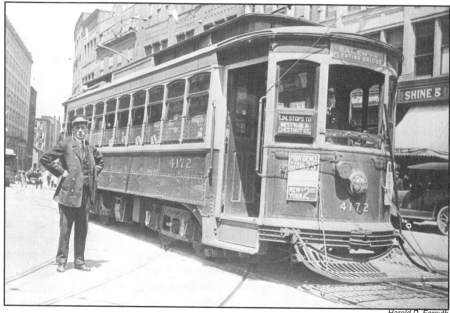

The Laconia Car Co. delivered 50 cars in 1914 which duplicated the earlier 4100s. Car 4172 is at Central Sq., Lynn, in 1917, bound for Salem via Floating Bridge. The 4100s served as the prototype for the closed car delivered to Lowell National Historical Park in 1987.

Harold D. Forsyth

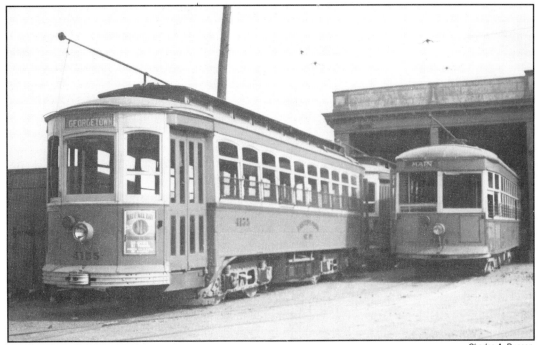

Charles A. Duncan

The changes in the carbuilding art in the eight years between the construction of 4155 and 6014, seen at Haverhill in 1936, are most obvious in the configuration of the roof. More important from the view of operating costs was the reduction in weight of some six tons.

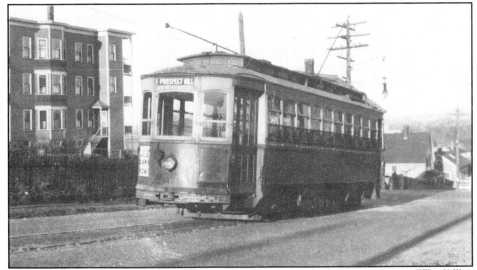

William H. Watts

In November 1932 semi-convertible 4173 operates on Lawrence's Prospect Hill route. The route would continue running until October 1934, nearly a year after the trolley had been scrapped.

Electing not to adopt the lease of the Newport lines, the Eastern Mass. in 1920 sold six 4100s to the Newport Electric Corp. They served the Rhode Island community until 1926, when they were sold to the Coast Cities Railway of Asbury Park, N.J. Car 703 is at North Long Branch, N.J., in September 1928. The system was abandoned in 1931, but 703 survived as a shed for 45 years to be acquired by the Seashore Trolley Museum in 1976 for restoration as Bay State 4175.

Carlson Collection

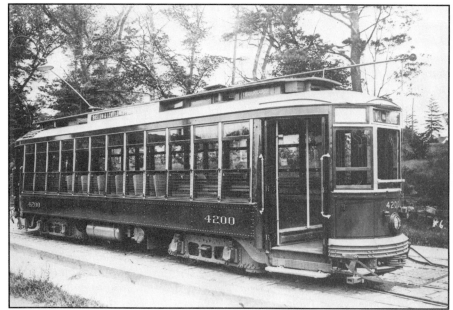

In 1915, under the leadership of Superintendent of Equipment E. W. Holst, the Bay State designed an experimental semi-convertible car. This prototype, numbered 4200, posed for its official portrait shortly after delivery from the Laconia Car Co. in the spring of 1915.

Bay State St.Ry., Duncan Collection

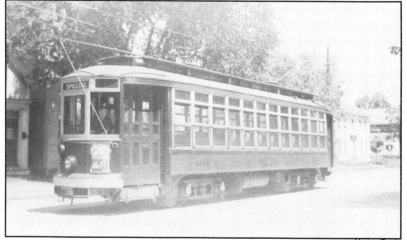

Subsequently renumbered 4100, the experimental car spent most of its life in Lynn and Revere. On June 16, 1935, it was transferred from Revere to Haverhill, in the process of which it had the distinction of making the last runs on the Salem–Lawrence and the Lawrence–Haverhill routes. It is shown here during that move on North St. in Salem.

Horton Banks

Harold D. Forsyth, Farrell Collection

Satisfied with 4200, the Bay State placed an order with Laconia for 200 similar cars on March 29, 1916. Car 4215 is on Humphrey St., Swampscott, in 1918.

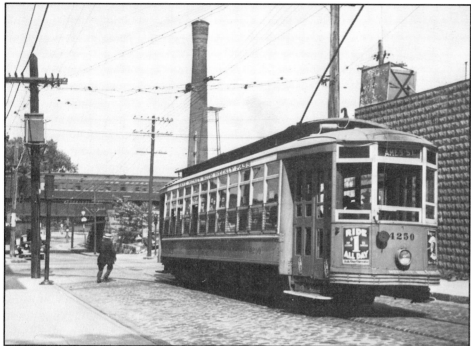

The 4200s were a mainstay of the system for two decades. Car 4250 was caught at Ames and Montello Sts., Brockton, in June 1937 with a New Haven passenger train in the background. All trolley service in Brockton ended on July 11, 1937.

Charles A. Duncan

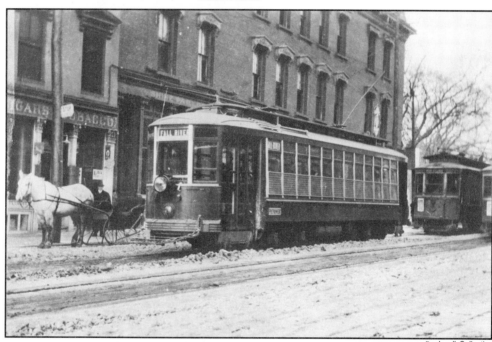

Car 4267 is seen shortly after delivery in Taunton. Note the horsedrawn open sleigh at the curb. In 1932 this car became the first of the class to be junked, and on July 9 of that year the last trolley line in Taunton was converted to buses.

Rockwell Collection

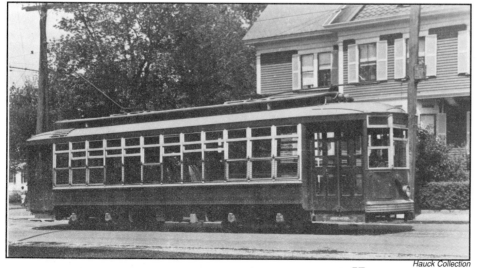

The 4300s differed from the 4200s in that they had multiple-unit control apparatus, although they never ran in trains. Car 4376 is in Lowell shortly before the September 8, 1935, conversion of that division to motor vehicle operation.

Hauck Collection

FROM SULLIVAN SQ. TO STONEHAM

ONE OF THE MOST PICTURESQUE trolley lines in the Bay State was the route between Sullivan Sq., Charlestown, and Stoneham through the Middlesex Fells Reservation. The Boston Elevated opened the segment from Sullivan Sq. to Spot Pond, Medford, on August 15, 1909, with the Boston & Northern commencing through service from Stoneham on April 16, 1910.

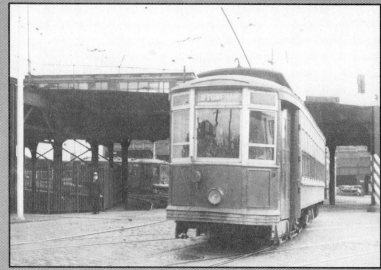

Charles A. Duncan

The route commenced at the Sullivan Sq. terminal of the Main Line Elevated. In this December 1935 view Eastern Mass. 4384 is about to follow Boston Elevated 5793 up the incline into the station. Elevated car 0336 can be seen on the structure above the two surface cars.

For most of its run through Medford, the line was in the center reservation of the Fellsway. Boston Elevated crews ran the cars on this portion of the route, conducting local business along the way. Boston-bound passengers board 4385 at the Fellway and Myrtle St. in June 1946. The sign on the car's dasher reads: "Save Your Selves—Let Us Be Your Chauffeur."

Stanley M. Hauck

Signed for Spot Pond, car 4385 (RIGHT) pauses at the Sheepfold in September 1938. The Sheepfold was the location where the change from Boston Elevated to Eastern Mass. crews took place. From that point, the route continued on private right-of-way through the Middlesex Fells Reservation. Car 4381 (BELOW) heads for Stoneham in December 1938.

Horton Banks

Charles A. Duncan

. . . THE FELLSWAY LINE

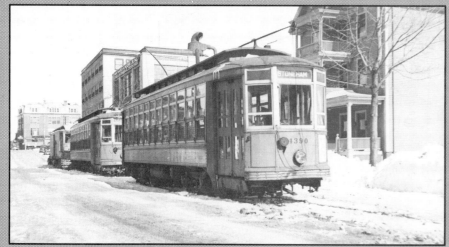

Three days after the St. Valentine's Day blizzard of 1940 car 4390 heads a lineup of cars on Main St. just to the south of Stoneham Sq.

Charles A. Duncan

The line extended beyond Stoneham Sq. to the point where the Boston & Maine's Stoneham Branch crossed the highway. Prior to December 1918 the tracks continued north to Reading. In February 1939 a railfan excursion (BELOW) saw BERy 5191 and EMSR 4381 at the end of track.

Horton Banks

The Eastern Mass. discontinued the Stoneham line on July 28, 1946, ending its last rail service north of Boston. The Boston Elevated and the successor MTA, however, continued to operate Type 5 cars such as 5529 along the Fellsway as far as Elm St., Medford, until December 17, 1955.

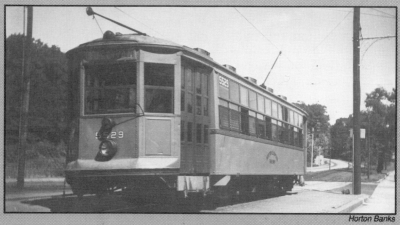

Horton Banks

Semi-convertible 4228 waits between trips on the Pleasant St. line at the Narrows in Fall River in April 1936. Note the "Ladies Entrance" to Dreamland, a sign of an era when it was not deemed proper for women to enter such establishments by the front door.

Charles A. Duncan

Horton Banks

U.S. Navy, Boston National Historical Park Collection

Car 4241 operates as a special car on the Houghs Neck line in Quincy in January 1940. Service on this route continued until June 30, 1946.

A Boston-bound 4200-type car pauses on Chelsea St. in Charlestown in July 1929 to allow a Boston Type 5 to turn into Bunker Hill St. Workers are demolishing the granite wall adjacent to the Ropewalk of the Boston Navy Yard to allow more light to reach the 1300-foot-long structure.

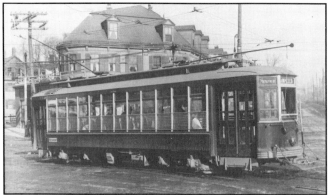

Boston Elevated Railway

Car 4285 leaves Mattapan Sq., Boston, for Brockton by way of Milton, Randolph, and Avon around 1918. This 14-mile route was abandoned in July 1930.

Except for a change from yellow to traction orange paint, the 4200s were little altered over the years. Nearing the end of its career, 4288 passes the "Narrow Gauge" railroad station in Lynn in December 1936.

Charles A. Duncan

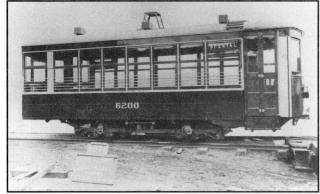

American Car Co., Duncan Collection

In 1917 the Bay State acquired a sample Birney safety car. Later renumbered 7000, it nears completion at the American Car Co. plant in St. Louis.

Harold D. Forsyth, Farrell Collection

The Eastern Mass. ordered 100 Birneys from Brill in August 1919, adding a second lot of 100 a month later and a final group of 50 early in 1920. Only Detroit had as many of the single-truck cars. Birney 5022 on the Christian Hill line in Lowell in 1922 attracts attention from neighborhood boys.

Theodore Santarelli de Brasch, Wonson Collection

The Birneys never totally met management expectations, and at no time were all in service. Eventually, some 80 cars were sold to other properties. Still, they had their place, as exemplified by 5086 in Chelsea Sq. in the 1930s. This car was one of seven Birneys sold to but not used by the Boston Elevated in 1936.

Horton Banks

Just as they were the final divisions to use 4100s, Fall River and Haverhill were the last to operate Birneys. Car 5133 waits for a passenger in downtown Haverhill on the last day of the Pines line, May 24, 1936.

61

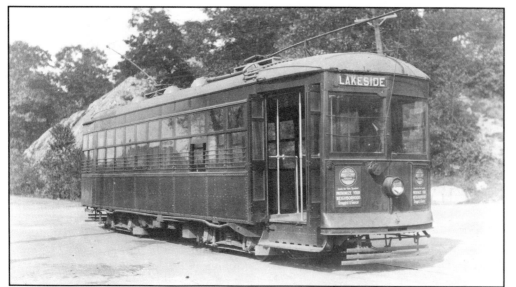

Harold D. Forsyth

In 1922 the Eastern Mass. acquired 25 lightweight cars from Brill. Shortly after delivery car 6022 was photographed on the Myrtle St. line in Lynn. An unusual feature of the cars was the lack of a rear door.

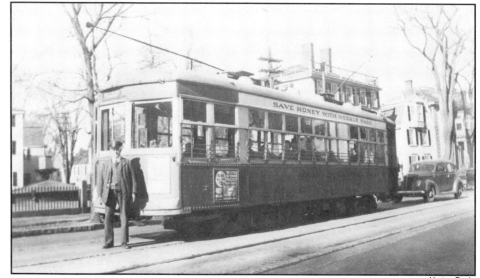

On the last day of rail service in Salem, February 28, 1937, the motorman poses for the photographer on Essex St. Slogans advertising various bargain fare plans were common on Eastern Mass. cars in later years.

Horton Banks

Charles A. Duncan

Car 6003 on South Main at Pleasant St., Fall River, in 1934 was one of eight 6000s sold to the Columbus & Southern Ohio Electric in 1936. They served the Buckeye State capital until 1947.

In March 1923 the Eastern Mass. placed an order with Brill for 50 lightweights. Built by Brill's subsidiary, G. C. Kuhlman of Cleveland, the new cars arrived in late 1923 and early 1924. Unlike the earlier 6000s, they had rear doors. Car 6041 from this lot is on the Campello line in Brockton in April 1936.

Horton Banks

Carlson Collection

A 6025-class car lays over in Cliftondale Sq., Saugus, in the mid-1930s. Until June 1920 the tracks continued around to the left and on through North Revere to Linden Sq., Malden, and a junction with Boston Elevated lines.

Charles A. Duncan

Car 6054 waits at McGaughey's turnout in Holbrook on the Quincy–Brockton line in February 1935. Service on this route would only continue until June 23, 1935.

In 1936 and 1937 a total of 30 of the 50 cars in the 6025 series were sold for further service in Brazil. One of those cars (RIGHT) is seen in 1950 as rebuilt into Companhia Carris Porto-Alegrense 25.

Morrison Collection

In 1927 EMSR received 50 cars differing but slightly from the previous lightweights. These two units passing on Winter St., East Saugus, in May 1936 illustrate what differences there were between 6055 of 1924 and 7016 of 1927, most notably in the area of the anticlimber.

Charles A. Duncan

A 7000-class car prepares to leave Saugus Center for Swampscott in early 1937. Service from here to Melrose Highlands was abandoned in November 1931. Of the structures in the picture, only the Civil War Monument survives in 1989.

Charles A. Duncan

The 7000s were built by both surviving Massachusetts car-builders—Osgood Bradley of Worcester and Wason of Springfield. Wason-built 7038 pauses for its portrait in Middleton Center in May 1935, three weeks before the end of service on the lengthy line between Lawrence and Salem.

Carlson Collection

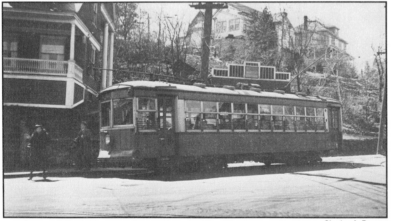

Car 7023 discharges passengers at the corner of Winter St. and Lincoln Ave., East Saugus, in April 1937. The Cliftondale line had the distinction of being the last operated by the Lynn division. At the time this view was exposed, 7023 had already been sold to the Boston Elevated, although it would not be delivered until after the end of rail service on June 7, 1937.

Charles A. Duncan

Nineteen years separated the construction of these two products of the Osgood Bradley plant, seen at Ship Yard Loop in Quincy. While Eastern Mass. 7004 of 1927 embodied the best of conventional rolling stock, Boston Elevated 3221 incorporated the results of 15 years of research and development by the transit industry to develop a truly modern streetcar capable of competing with the motor bus.

William V. Kenney, Hauck Collection

Charles A. Brown

The Quincy division was the last to operate streetcars. In the final years 7000s provided all base service. The premier route of the division ran from Quincy Sq. to Fields Corner, Boston, with a change of crews at Neponset Loop. This June 1938 view of 7012 there reveals how the companies kept revenue accounting simple by changing fareboxes with the motormen.

Lightweight 7035 of 1927 and ACF 36-S bus 1061 of 1939 pose together in Quincy Sq. in September 1947, about eight months before the end of rail service.

Stanley M. Hauck

Rockwell Collection

The last Eastern Mass. cars operated in the United States were the 7000s sold to the Boston Elevated and the Birmingham Electric Co. in 1936 and 1937. The Birmingham group was extensively rebuilt into single-end Peter Witt-style cars. Birmingham 584 carries an advertisement for the 1946 M-G-M release, *The Mighty McGurk*, starring Wallace Beery (note the error on the sign) as it serves the Travelick line. Both Boston and Birmingham sold the second-hand EMSR units for scrap in 1950.

A COLOR PORTFOLIO

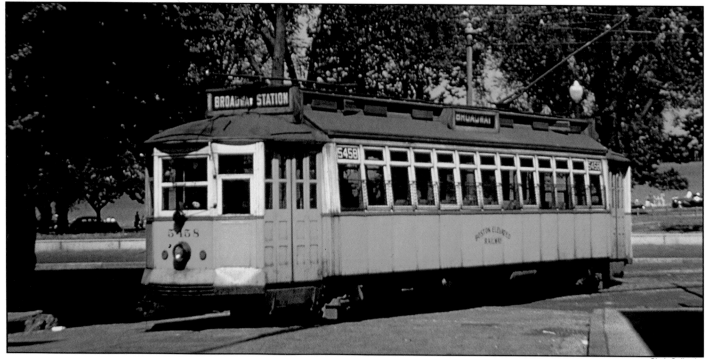

Boston Elevated Railway Type 4 no. 5458 sits at Farragut Rd. in South Boston in early July 1945. Placed in service on June 3, 1914, the Jewett Car Co. product remained on the property until 1949. This extension of the City Point lines was a summer-only operation.

Boston's Reservoir carhouse was a scene of change in September 1948. PCC cars were replacing center-entrance cars on Beacon St. and Commonwealth Ave. Center-entrance car 6156 is nearly lost amid the streamliners. The tan roof on PCC 3097 was ostensibly a blackout measure applied to the earliest "Wartime" PCCs. Boston Elevated records, however, reveal that the real reason for the "tan tops" was the unavailability of aluminum paint.

In the 1890s Massachusetts could boast that it was home to at least eight carbuilders. By the 1980s, there were none left in the entire United States, and the MBTA awarded the contract for its Type 7 surface rail cars to Kinki Sharyo of Osaka, Japan. In June 1988 car 3661 makes the loop through the Riverside carhouse yard.

On the last morning of service on the Washington Street Elevated, April 30, 1987, a four-car train of No. 12 Main Line rapid transit cars pauses at Egleston on its way to Forest Hills.

On April 20, 1946, Eastern Mass. Street Railway semi-convertible 4397 pauses to change operators at the Sheepfold. The Fellsway line was the last stronghold of the nearly 30-year-old cars. Sister unit 4387 is preserved at the Seashore Trolley Museum.

The newest cars in the Eastern Mass. fleet, the 7000s ruled the Quincy division from the late 1930s until the end of rail service. Bradley-built 7004 on the Ship Yard run is at Quincy Sq. in October 1947.

This view of Union Street Railway 273 leaves no doubt why units of this class were known as "Yellow Belly" cars. Built by Jones in 1912, it was among the last of its type in service in the Whaling City.

The most modern cars in New Bedford were the Osgood Bradley "Electromobiles" of 1929. During World War II, the USR, like many transit operators, painted a unit in patriotic colors, as this August 1945 view attests.

Lawson K. Hill

Lightweight cars of different properties exhibited many small differences even when constructed by the same builder. Compare Worcester Street Railway 588, seen at Green Hill Park in September 1945, with Eastern Mass. 7004 on page 68. Both had been built by Osgood Bradley in 1927.

A key element in the revitalization of Lowell in the 1970s and '80s has been the creation of the Lowell National Historical Park. To connect the various mills and canals comprising the site, the National Park Service strung wire over a railroad spur track and commissioned the construction of two 15-bench open streetcars. The first opens built for domestic service in some six decades, they were based on the Old Colony/Bay State 1597-1600 series and utilized mechanical equipment from scapped Melbourne, Australia, trams. Cars 1601 and 1602 meet on Dutton St. in the summer of 1986.

Stephen P. Carlson

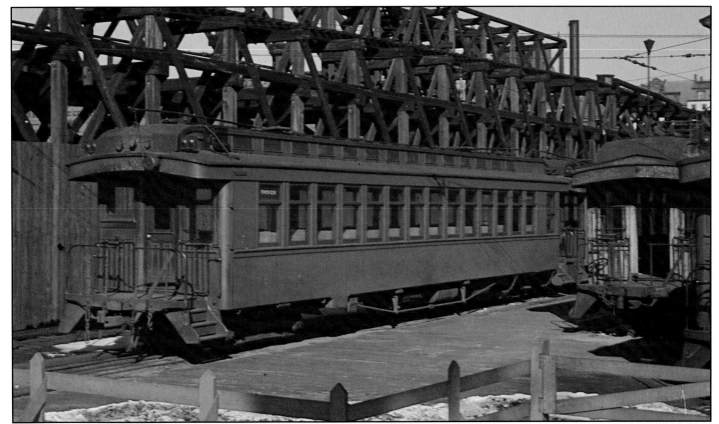

Ellis Spear, 470 Railroad Club Collection

The Boston, Revere Beach & Lynn did not purchase new rolling stock for its electrification in 1928. Rather, it reequipped its Laconia-built wooden coaches with special Brill narrow-gauge motor trucks and multiple-unit control. One such motor car sits at the East Boston ferry terminal of the "Narrow Gauge."

Not all of Massachusetts' electric transit vehicles rode on steel wheels on rails. At its peak, the Boston area had the nation's fifth-largest trackless trolley network. The destination sign on "Gray Ghost" trolley coach 8522, a 1951 Pullman-Standard product, on a fantrip at the Cambridge Common in November 1967 serves as a reminder of the period from 1948 to 1962 when the electric buses ruled the surface lines in Dorchester.

Bradley H. Clarke

Streetcars far outnumber automobiles in this late 1910s view of Main St., Springfield. The Springfield Street Railway was one of five Massachusetts lines controlled by the New England Investment & Security Co., a subsidiary of the New York, New Haven & Hartford Railroad.

NEW HAVEN OWNED

WORCESTER, SPRINGFIELD & BERKSHIRE

UNDER PRESIDENT CHARLES S. MELLEN, the New York, New Haven & Hartford Railroad pursued a policy of monopolizing rail transportation in southern New England. The New Haven's interest in acquiring electric railways had begun prior to his ascendency to the presidency in 1903, but reached its apex under his leadership.

Although more nearly attaining its desired goal in Connecticut and Rhode Island, the New Haven's street railway holdings in Massachusetts were extensive. Between 1905 and 1910 it acquired companies having approximately 20 percent of the trackage in the Bay State. As finally constituted, there were three major and two minor operating companies. Total consolidation of the properties into one firm was never achieved because the General Court failed to override Governor Eugene Foss' 1912 veto of a bill to create the Worcester, Springfield & Berkshire Street Railway.

In a 1913 interview with the Boston *Sunday Post*, Mellen explained that the New Haven was "in the electric railway buisness because the electrical lines are natural feeders of traffic to the main road." In the same interview he opposed the projected Boston & Providence Interurban because it paralleled the railroad's route between those two points. Thus, he stated the principal underlying reason for its activities: the elimination of "direct competitors of the New Haven."

At the same time Mellen blamed the railroad's legal troubles in the commonwealth on Boston Elevated and other Boston-area interests, a charge not totally without merit. (Governor Foss, for example, had been a director of the Massachusetts Electric Companies, parent firm of the Bay State Street Railway.) But business rivalry was not the sole reason, for the New Haven's actions violated a 1906 law forbidding railroads from "directly or indirectly" acquiring other corporations without legislative consent.

That the road's street railways were in the hands of a holding company, the New England Investment & Security Co., headquartered in Springfield, did not shield it from prosecution. In 1909 the Massachusetts Supreme Judicial Court ordered the divestiture of its trolley properties, a ruling repeated by a federal district court five years later. But the New Haven was not without its political influence; the court orders were never enforced, and indeed the General Court in 1915 validated its holdings. Finally, in 1927 the railroad was permitted to assume direct control of the streetcar systems. Not until 1958 did it sell the Berkshire, the last of its street railways in the state.

THE LARGEST of the New Haven properties, the Worcester Consolidated Street Railway had been formed in 1887 by the merger of the Worcester and the Citizens Street Railways. The former line had been in business since 1869, while the latter was but two years old. Trolleys appeared on September 2, 1891, and in a little over two years totally replaced the horsecar.

A considerable network of suburban lines grew up around the commonwealth's second-largest city. The Worcester, Leicester & Spencer was built in 1891, becoming the Worcester & Suburban in 1895, at the same time absorbing the Worcester & Millbury. The Worcester & Suburban became part of the Worcester Consolidated in 1901 along with the Worcester & Marlborough and the Leominster & Clinton. This last firm was itself a product of mergers, encompassing the Worcester & Clinton, the Fitchburg & Suburban, and the Clinton & Hudson.

In 1901 the Worcester & Southbridge Street Railway commenced operation on its route west from the city toward Southbridge and Sturbridge. The New Haven acquired the Worcester & Southbridge five years later, shortly after the railroad had gained control of the Worcester Consolidated. The final corporate mergers came in May 1911 as the WCSR absorbed the Worcester & Southbridge, the Marlborough & Westborough (chartered in 1896), the Worcester & Holden (opened in 1903), and the Worcester & Blackstone Valley, a line built in 1897 running southeast to the Rhode Island state line. In addition, the firm controlled the Webster & Dudley Street Railway through a lease arrangement.

The 1910s and early '20s were the peak years for the railway. Its lines radiated north to Holden; northeast to Leominster and Fitchburg by way of both Sterling and Clinton; east to Hudson and Marlborough through Shrewsbury and Westborough; southeast to Blackstone and Woonsocket, R.I.; south to Webster and the Connecticut line; and west to Springfield via Sturbridge and to Spencer.

Track mileage fell off rapidly after the initial abandonments in 1924. The lengthy Springfield, Fitchburg, and Blackstone services went in 1927, and by 1931 the system was largely confined to the city of Worcester and was in receivership. Sold to the New England Gas & Electric Association and reorganized as the Worcester Street Railway in June 1932, the system turned away from electric transit. Most of the lighter lines were replaced with buses in the mid-1930s, and plans were adopted for a total conversion by 1942.

While the DPU issued the last state certificates of conven-

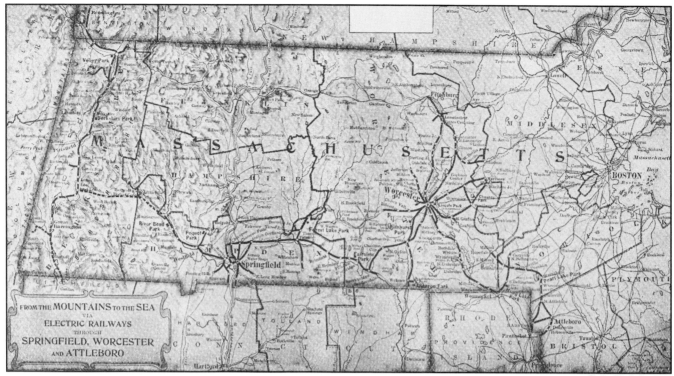

Trolley Wayfinder, *1911*

A 1911 publicity map shows the geographic extent of the New Haven Railroad's street railway holdings in Massachusetts.

ience needed to run the replacement buses in January 1941, the final conversion would not occur until December 31, 1945, as first the shortage of buses and then federal wartime prohibitions on trolley replacement delayed the changeover.

LOCATED ON THE CONNECTICUT RIVER some 60 miles west of Worcester, Springfield saw its first horsecar run on March 9, 1870. Slightly more than 20 years later, on June 9, 1890, the first electric cars began operation on the Forest Park route. As in other cities, the elimination of equine motive power occurred as rapidly as economically possible. The Springfield Street Railway's last horsecar ran on January 9, 1893.

In 1905 the New Haven gained control of the railway, along with the Springfield & Eastern, a company formed in 1897 as the Palmer & Monson Street Railway. Actual merger of the two lines did not occur until December 1910, although an operating lease had effectively combined them five years earlier.

The other consolidation, occurring in 1909, had involved the Western Massachusetts Street Railway. Extending west through Westfield to Huntington, that firm had been chartered in 1904 and had absorbed the Woronoco Street Railway three years later.

The system connected with the Hartford & Springfield to the south, the Worcester Consolidated and the Warren, Brookfield & Spencer to the east, and the Holyoke Street Railway to the north. The last of these interurban lines was the Springfield–Holyoke route, converted to buses on September 6, 1935.

Cutbacks in rail service began with abandonment of the Wason Ave. spur in 1918 and accelerated in the mid- to late 1920s, with all local service in Westfield and Palmer ending in 1927. A decade later, all trolley operation had ceased west of the Connecticut River.

The sale of the company to the City Coach Co. in 1939 was accompanied by the announcement that the system would be all-bus by the end of 1941. It did not take that long. Four lines went

in 1939, and between May 11 and June 22, 1940, the last nine routes were abandoned. The newest cars, however, were to labor on in places such as Montreal, Norfolk, and Birmingham.

THE THIRD MAJOR NEW HAVEN SYSTEM, the Berkshire Street Railway, was chartered in June 1902 to build a route from North Adams to the Connecticut state line at Great Barrington by way of Pittsfield. It opened in 1905, the same year that the New Haven obtained control of the company.

The road was not the first in Massachusetts' westernmost county. In 1886 the Hoosac Valley Street Railway began horse-car service in the Adams-North Adams area, while the Pittsfield Street Railway began operations in that community. Those lines were electrified in 1889 and 1891, respectively.

The New Haven gained control of the Hoosac Valley in early 1906, merging it into the Berkshire on June 30 of that year. Four years later a bitter rivalry ended when the Berkshire absorbed the Pittsfield Electric, successor to the Pittsfield Street Railway.

In March 1912 the Berkshire leased the Vermont Company, formalizing a relationship that had existed since the New Haven had purchased the predecessor Bennington & North Adams Street Railway in 1906.

At its peak the Berkshire provided service from Hoosick Falls, N.Y., through Bennington, Vt., North Adams, Pittsfield, Lee, and Great Barrington, Mass., to Canaan, Ct. It also briefly operated a line east from Lee to Huntington, where it met, but had no physical link to, the Springfield Street Railway.

That service was abandoned in October 1918, and a year later operation from Great Barrington to Canaan ended. The Vermont Company lease was cancelled in 1922, and in 1929 the through route to Bennington quit. By late 1930 all but the Pittsfield lines had been abandoned. They lasted only two more years, the final one going on November 12, 1932.

THE TWO SMALLER NEW HAVEN LINES operated in the geographical area between Worcester, Attleborough, and the Rhode Island state line. Indeed, the Milford, Attleborough & Woonsocket Street Railway was primarily a bridge route. Incorporated in 1898, it provided a link in the chain of New Haven properties between the Worcester Consolidated and the Rhode Island Co. at Woonsocket and the Interstate Consolidated at Plainville. It also connected with the Milford & Uxbridge at Milford, the Dedham & Franklin at Franklin, and the Norton, Taunton & Attleborough at Wrentham. Operated in conjunction with the Interstate Consolidated, it was never a heavily-patronized line and was abandoned in 1924.

The Attleborough, North Attleborough & Wrentham Street Railway was chartered in 1889. Six years later, it became a part of the Interstate Consolidated Street Railway of Providence, R.I. In 1901 a new Interstate Consolidated was incorporated under Massachusetts law to take over the Rhode Island firm's holdings in the Bay State, and two years later the road took over the trackage of the Attleborough Branch Railroad.

For most of its existence, the Interstate Consolidated, which connected Attleborough and Providence via Pawtucket, R.I., was operated as a division of its parent firm, the Rhode Island Co. Through service ended in 1918, and six years later the company went into receivership. Emerging in the mid-1920s as the Interstate Street Railway, it modernized its facilities and struggled on for the remainder of the decade. Service to Pawtucket ended in December 1931, and in June 1933 the remainder of the system was abandoned.

The Millbury Town Hall serves as a backdrop for cars 31 and 32 of the Worcester & Millbury Street Railway. Opened in 1892, the line merged into the Worcester & Suburban Street Railway in January 1895.

Wonson Collection

The Worcester & Clinton Street Railway opened in 1898 connecting the two named points by way of Boylston, and formed one leg of the original route between Worcester and Leominster. Along with several other lines radiating from Clinton, it was absorbed by the Leominster & Clinton in 1900 and the Worcester Consolidated a year later. Car 19 is on Front St. in Worcester.

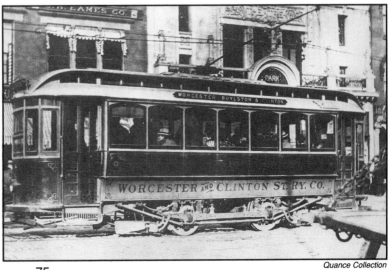

Quance Collection

Ten-bench open 183 was one of 10 such cars built for the Worcester Consolidated by the local Osgood Bradley Co. in 1898. Bradley, which began to construct railroad cars in the 1830s, built a large portion of its home town's trolley fleet. The last of a large number of carbuilders in the state, Bradley became a part of Pullman-Standard in 1930 and remained in business until 1960.

Quance Collection

Prior to the passage of a state law in 1900 mandating the vestibuling of streetcars for winter service, the motorman was exposed to the elements. Thus, motormen wore heavier coats than did their conductors, as this view of WCSR 23 demonstrates. Note the off-center end door on the unit, which may have been the product of the Brownell Car Co. of St. Louis.

Clark Collection

The Worcester & Webster Street Railway was formed in 1898. Its 18.3-mile route linked Worcester with the Connecticut Co. at North Grosvenordale, Ct. The line also served Beacon Park, which attracted a large number of excursion car operations such as this one using 12-bench open 10. Leased by the Worcester & Southbridge in 1906 and the Worcester Consolidated after 1911, the line was abandoned in 1926.

Clark Collection

Worcester & Suburban 157 was one of four half-open cars built in 1900 by Wason. They were converted to full open cars a year later since, as the *Electric Railway Journal* reported, "it was found that passengers were willing to ride inside only when it was too cold to stay outside."

Wason, Carlson Collection

In 1902 Osgood Bradley delivered the parlor car "Huguenot" to the Worcester & Southbridge. Shortly after its arrival, it posed at Pinehurst Park. The elaborately-finished car even had its own dishes and silverware. After being taken over by the Worcester Consolidated in 1911, it was slightly altered by Wason and saw service on both Worcester and Springfield rails. It was scrapped around 1927.

Brock Collection

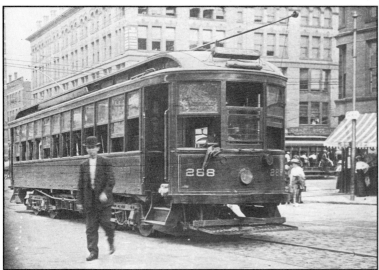

Quance Collection

In 1904 Bradley turned out four closed cars with 34-foot 1-inch bodies for suburban service. Signed for Spencer, car 288 is at Salem Sq. in downtown Worcester.

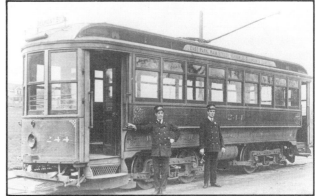

Phillips Collection

A year earlier, the Worcester carbuilder had supplied 14 cars of 25-foot length for city service.

A November 1940 railfan excursion brought sand car 809 out of the Market St. carhouse for the benefit of photographers. Built by Wason in 1909 as car 23 of the Worcester & Blackstone Valley Street Railway, it was one of the last two surviving cars acquired from the Consolidated's underlying companies.

C. L. Siebert

Stephenson-built car 409 of 1907 follows American Car Sprinkler Co. 160 north on Main St. The American Car Sprinkler Co. was a Worcester-based firm supplying its services to street railways throughout New England and eastern New York.

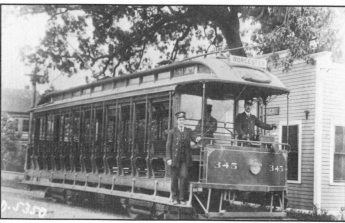

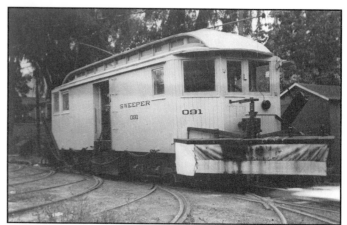

Car 345 (ABOVE) on Main St., Shrewsbury, around 1910 was one of 16 opens built for the Worcester Consolidated by Laconia in 1900. Eleven of these 14-bench units were rebuilt into snow sweepers for both Worcester and Springfield after the cessation of open service. Springfield 091 (ABOVE RIGHT) was the former WCSR 346, while Worcester 07 (RIGHT), shown in action on Vernon in March 1937, was formerly no. 348.

In 1907 Stephenson completed an order for 15-bench opens. The lead unit of this 14-car group operates in Monument Sq., Leominster, in 1912. During 1918 they were rebuilt by Bradley as closed cars.

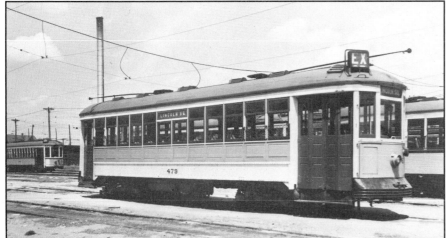

In 1914 the WCSR received a group of 10 semi-steel convertible cars from Bradley. Known locally as "Fifth Avenue Cars" because of their resemblence to contemporary New York equipment, they were scrapped in 1938. No. 479 exhibits the chrome yellow paint scheme adopted in 1916.

Wonson Collection

Between 1916 and 1918 the railway took delivery of 21 arch-roof steel cars for city service. Car 481 waits to depart Salem Sq. for Spencer around 1920.

Quance Collection

E. B. Luce, DeCelle Collection

One of 10 Birneys constructed for the Worcester Consolidated by Bradley in 1920, car 543 poses for its portrait on Salisbury St. at Lincoln Sq.

Charles A. Duncan, Hill Collection

E. C. Piercy, Morrison Collection

The 10 lightweight cars acquired from Bradley in 1924 used numbers previously assigned to open cars. In 1943 nos. 518 and 519 of this series (LEFT) pass on Park Ave. at Maywood. Two years later the entire class was sold to Salvador, Bahia State, Brazil, where they were renumbered 501-510. Car 505 (RIGHT) is seen in the Brazilian city in 1953.

Roger Borrup, Wonson Collection

In 1927 the Worcester Consolidated purchased 50 lightweights from Bradley, the last new streetcars built for the property. In September 1935 two of these cars, operating on routes 8 *Salisbury* and 1 *Providence,* meet in front of the old Union Station.

Lightweight 588 loads at a safety zone on Main St. in early 1938. The cars displayed the route number in the right front window instead of in the separate sign box on the roof used by earlier Worcester units.

Richard L. Wonson

Clark Collection

Car 563 passes under the Boston & Albany Railroad on Grafton St. at Washington Sq.

Charles A. Duncan

In May 1937 no. 589 heads inbound from the end of the Summit line. Service on this route ended later that year.

WORCESTER–SPRINGFIELD THROUGH SERVICE

FROM 1907 to 1927 the Worcester Consolidated and the Springfield Street Railways operated a through service between Salem Sq., Worcester, and Court Sq., Springfield, through Southbridge, Sturbridge, Brim-field, and Palmer. The 57.6-mile-long line was the longest trolley run in New England, requiring 3 hours each way. Equipment of both properties alternated on the line, a practice which continued long after buses had replaced streetcars.

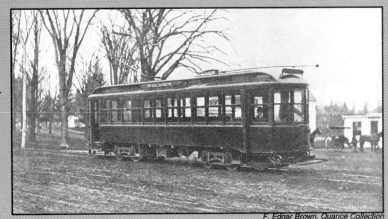

F. Edgar Brown, Quance Collection

The caption on this postcard reads "First Electric Passenger Car into Brimfield, Mass., May 6, 1907."

Cummings Collection

In 1913 a group of ten 35-foot semi-steel cars with 65-hp. motors and HLF control were acquired for the line. Six cars were the property of the Worcester Consolidated, while four were carried on the books of the Springfield Street Railway. Springfield 462 is on Main St. in its home city.

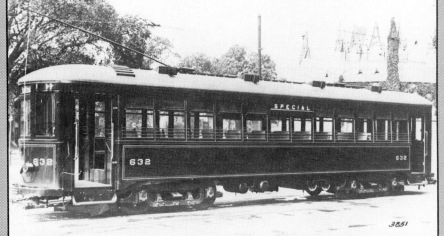

Newly-arrived from the Wason factory, one of Worcester's share of the joint order poses for its official portrait at Memorial Sq., Springfield.

Springfield St. Ry., Brock Collection

Horsecar 32 of the Springfield Street Railway is on Walnut St. in 1888. Like most early streetcars, the route designations painted on the car limited it to the one service.

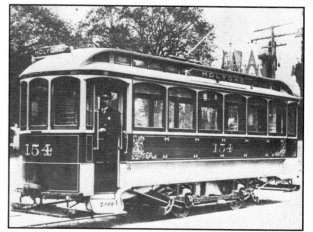

On July 25, 1895, the Springfield Street Railway made a connection with the Holyoke Street Railway at Riley Brook. Single-truck car 154 in front of the company's office building at Memorial Sq. carries signs for Holyoke Service.

Many early cars ended their careers as service equipment. The operating crew relaxes while sand car 094 (ex-182) is loaded through one of its windows in October 1936.

The first double-truck car on the Springfield system was produced by Wason in 1892 by splicing together the bodies of Jones-built horsecars 41 and 42. Here the resultant unit is painted for duty on the Chicopee route.

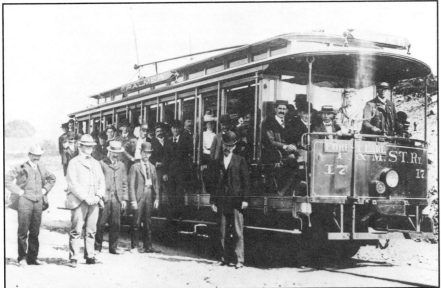

The Palmer & Monson Street Railway was organized in 1897 to link its two namesake communities. Four years later, it changed its name to the Springfield & Eastern. Coming under New Haven control, it merged into the Springfield Street Railway in 1910. The occasion for this photograph of 13-bench open 17 was the opening of the Ware line to Palmer via Forest Lake in July 1900.

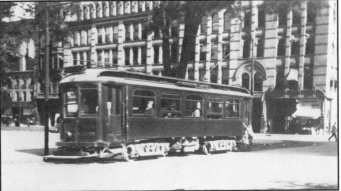

The MCB-style trucks on Western Mass. 104 at Court Sq., Springfield, are indicative of the interurban nature of the line.

The Western Massachusetts Street Railway was incorporated in late 1904 to build a line westward from Westfield to Huntington. The first car into Huntington was 14-bench open 109.

The crew of Woronoco Street Railway car 10 poses for the photographer. The line, serving Westfield, was founded in 1890 and became part of the Western Massachusetts in 1907, two years before the Western Mass. itself was absorbed by the Springfield system.

The Hartford & Springfield Street Railway provided through service between Springfield and Hartford, Ct. The Springfield Street Railway operated the cars within Massachusetts and provided some of the rolling stock for the service, which lasted from January 1902 until early 1926. Springfield Street Railway 287 is at State and Main in Hartford on August 31, 1904.

In September 1935 car 331 meets a Holyoke Street Railway car at the West Springfield (Riverdale) division point. Through service between Springfield and Holyoke was discontinued on September 6, 1936. Service from Springfield to the Holyoke city line continued for another year.

Pitt Holland, Hill Collection

The Wason Manufacturing Co. had been established in 1845 and became a subsidiary of J. G. Brill in 1906. Renamed Brill of Massachusetts in 1931, the Springfield plant officially closed its doors in April 1932. The tower of the firm's office building appears in many of its builder's photographs, including this 1895 view of Springfield's parlor car "Rockcrimmon," resplendent in blue livery with gold trim. Retired in 1918, the car would not be scrapped for another decade.

Wason, Clark Collection

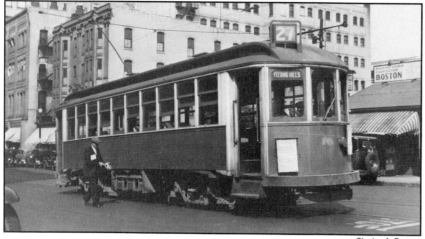

Charles A. Duncan

Wooden suburban car 380 at Vernon and Broadway is on the Feeding Hills line. That service was abandoned in November 1936. The building to the right of the trolley housed the Peter Pan Bus Lines.

Like many other properties, the Springfield Street Railway rebuilt open cars into closed vehicles. Several of those units were later converted to work equipment. Service car 0102, built by Wason in 1910 as passenger car 460, sits at the Hooker St. yard in October 1939.

Horton Banks

Suburban car 454 operates on the Indian Orchard line two weeks before its conversion to buses in May 1940. This car was one of the last two into the barn on June 23, 1940, to end railway service.

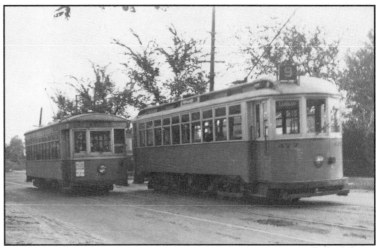

The last wooden suburban cars were acquired in 1913. Car 477 of that lot passes lightweight 567 on Page Blvd. in September 1936.

Common management of the Springfield and Worcester properties meant that simultaneous orders were placed for rolling stock. Compare Wason-built convertible 489 with Worcester Consolidated 479 on page 79.

In 1919 and 1920 the SSR acquired 20 Birneys. Car 536 of the second group is fresh from the builder's shop. The last of these one-man safety cars was withdrawn in 1932.

Arched roof steel cars were purchased in the late 1910s. Car 507 is on the private right-of-way of the Hamburg line in October 1939.

In 1923 Wason delivered 10 cars to Springfield which were the longest operated in western Massachusetts. Car 549 is at Chicopee Falls in 1935. Nos. 544-553 became Birmingham Electric Co. 300-309 in 1941. After rebuilding by Perley Thomas into single-end cars, they labored for another decade in the Alabama steel city.

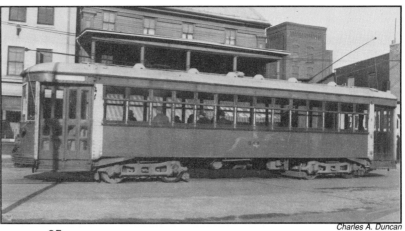

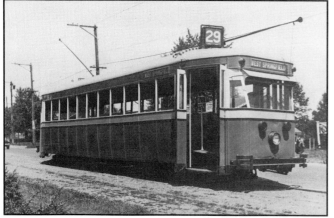

In early 1927 Springfield took delivery of one of only two "truly revolutionary" streetcars built in the 1920s and early 1930s. Featuring aluminum and steel construction, it rode on roller-bearing trucks and had Timken worm gear drive and "automotive-type" motors, with "remote" control. Total weight was just under 12 tons. Except for a tendency to derail on some lines, Springfield 554 was a success and a significant step along the road that would produce the PCC car. Nicknamed "Miss Springfield," it operates at West Springfield in August 1935. It ran regularly on route 29 from July 1935 until the abandonment of that line in November 1936. Otherwise, it shared the fate of most experimental units for most of its life—resting at the back of the yard.

Donald E. Shaw, DeCelle Collection

Unable to wait until 554 had been thoroughly tested, Springfield in 1927 ordered 50 lightweight cars from Wason. They differed only in detail from the cars built by Bradley for Worcester at the same time. In March 1940 car 573 is on Lyman St. at Springfield Union Station operating on the 4 *St. James Ave.* line.

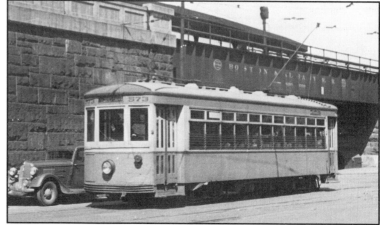

Charles A. Brown

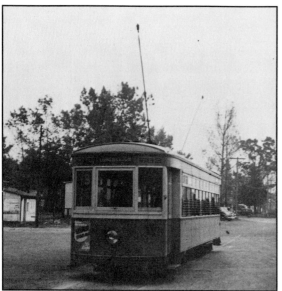

Charles A. Brown

In October 1938 car 582 changes ends at the outer terminal of the Longmeadow line.

Horton Banks

Service on route 3 *King St.* ended on November 19, 1939. A month before the end, lightweight 567 is outbound on the line.

With the end of streetcar service, Springfield sold 10 lightweights to the Virginia Electric & Power Co. for service in Norfolk, Va., and another 39 to the Montreal Tramways. Following the end of rail service in the Quebec city, MTC 2056 (ex-SSR 575) was retired to the Warehouse Point Trolley Museum just down the Connecticut River from its original home.

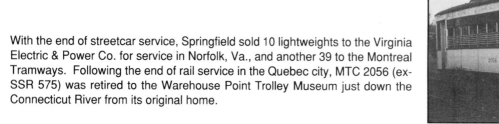

Laurence M. Blanke, Jr.

Cummings Collection, NHRHTA Archives

The Hoosac Valley Street Railway did not acquire its first open horsecars until two years after its October 1886 opening. One of those cars (RIGHT) passes the Adams Town Hall. The line was electrified using the Thomson-Houston system and four closed cars built by Newburyport. Shortly after the opening of the line from Zylonite carhouse to North Adams in October 1889, car 1 (ABOVE), named "Renfrew," rounds the corner at Main and State Sts., North Adams.

Cummings Collection, NHRHTA Archives

The Pittsfield Street Railway, in debt since its opening in 1886, was sold to the Pittsfield Electric Street Railway in 1890. In July 1891 that road commenced electrified service. In mid-1896 the company opened a line to the neighboring town of Dalton, home of Crane Paper, then as now contractor for federal currency stock. During the following winter, 20-foot closed car 20 stops on Main St. at the Dalton Town Hall. The 1896 Stephenson product was renumbered 42 in 1908 and became Berkshire Street Railway 108 after the acquisition of the Pittsfield Electric by the Berkshire in 1910.

Cummings Collection, NHRHTA Archives

Although street railway accidents were common throughout the trolley era, none had the potential national consequences of the one which occurred shortly after this photograph was taken by a *Berkshire Eagle* photographer in Pittsfield on September 3, 1902. Pittsfield Electric 29 struck the carriage carrying President Theodore Roosevelt and Governor W. Murray Crane. Both men were thrown from their vehicle, as was Secret Service agent William Craig (seated to the right of the driver), who was killed instantly. In the aftermath of what T.R. termed "a damned outrage," motorman Euclid Madden pleaded guilty to manslaughter and spent six months in the Berkshire County House of Correction.

The Berkshire Street Railway opened its line north from Pittsfield to Cheshire on June 23, 1902, and the route south to Great Barrington in stages between August and November. The initial rolling stock included 15 cars with 35-foot 8-inch bodies built by Wason. Car 26 of that lot is at Housatonic, a location which typifies the rural trolley line through Massachusetts' westernmost county.

PARLOR CARS

From 1909 to 1913 the Berkshire Street Railway boasted two parlor cars. The "Bennington" (LEFT) had been converted from passenger car 56 in 1909. The 1906 Laconia product had been transferred from another New Haven property, the Western Massachusetts, and would be returned to Springfield in 1916, where it resumed its original number of 100. The "Berkshire Hills" (RIGHT) was built in 1903 by Wason, and, in the words of historian O. R. Cummings, was "the most resplendent of the trolley parlor cars in New England."

The 24-mile line from East Lee to Huntington, which featured many steep grades as it crossed the Berkshires, opened in its entirety on August 15, 1917. On that date, combination car 162, a 1911 Bradley product, is the object of much interest as it waits at the end of track. The Berkshire suspended service on this route in October 1918 for the winter months. It subsequently declined to reopen it after a request for a local subsidy to cover operating losses was rejected.

Cummings Collection, NHRHTA Archives

Cummings Collection, NHRHTA Archives

Berkshire Valuation Co., Wonson Collection

The standard open cars of the Berkshire were vestibule-front, railroad roof units, with from 13 to 15 benches. One of the 14-bench cars (LEFT) is in Canaan, Ct. To comply with the state's reduced step height regulations, the BSR converted the majority of its open fleet, including 83 (RIGHT), to end-entrance, center-aisle cars in 1916. Most other firms opted for the less expensive solution of adding an extra running board.

Harold D. Forsyth, Duncan Collection

Car 142, a 25-foot unit constructed by Jones in 1910, was one of the few pieces of Berkshire rolling stock not built by Wason. It was in dead storage by 1923.

In 1919 the Berkshire ordered 17 Birney cars, but received only five, the others being diverted to the Connecticut Co. They were replaced by a group of Birneys delivered in 1920 and assigned to local lines in Pittsfield. Car 223, in the chrome yellow livery which replaced the earlier olive green colors in the 1920s, is on Dalton Ave. at Benedict Rd. It was scrapped along with the majority of the Birneys in 1930.

Raymond M. Sawyer, Cummings Collection, NHRHTA Archives

THE 300 CLASS

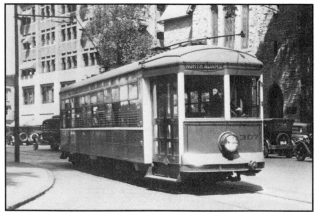

Wonson Collection

Cummings Collection, NHRHTA Archives

In October 1926 the Berkshire received a dozen lightweight cars from Osgood Bradley. Car 307 (ABOVE) at Pittsfield is signed for North Adams, while 310 (ABOVE RIGHT) is at Dry Bridge switch in Glendale bound for Great Barrington in September 1929. With the abandonment of railway service by the Berkshire in 1932, the lightweights were sold to another New Haven property, the Connecticut Co. They spent 16 years on the New Haven division. Car 3204 (ex-BSR 304) (RIGHT) is at the railroad station in New Haven.

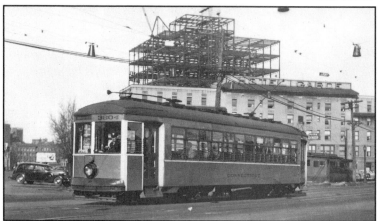

Harding Collection

Milford, Attleborough & Woonsocket Street Railway

B. J. Persons, Rockwell Collection

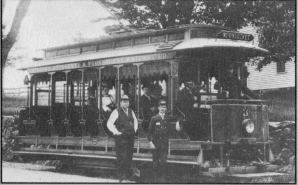

Cummings Collection

Clark Collection

The MA&W's line from Milford to Attleborough passed through Wrentham. Single-truck closed car 15 (ABOVE) is at Wrentham Common and the Congregational church in this pre-1906 postcard view. Bound for Woonsocket, Laconia-built 10-bench open 3 (ABOVE RIGHT) poses for the photographer in 1900. Around 1912 15-bench open 9 and 10-bench car 4 (RIGHT) wait on Mill St. in Attleborough for a trip to Plainville.

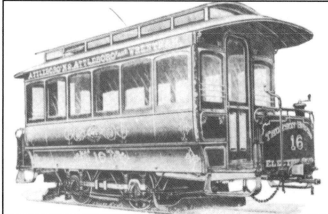

Attleborough, North Attleborough & Wrentham Street Railway car 16 was featured in an 1891 Ellis Car Co. advertisement in the *Street Railway Journal*.

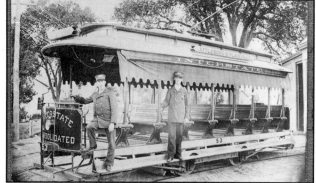

Eight-bench open 53 of the Interstate Consolidated Street Railway carries signs for the Attleborough–Plainville route, a run entirely within the commonwealth.

For most of its existence, the Interstate Consolidated used equipment of its parent firm, the Rhode Island Co. In addition to inheriting Rhode Island Co. cars, the successor Interstate Street Railway in 1924 purchased five lightweight cars from Wason. Two years later, lightweight 113 poses at the carbarn with ex-RICo 1022, one of the few Cincinnati-built streetcars to operate in Massachusetts.

In 1926 two additional lightweights were added to the roster. After the system was abandoned in 1933, car 122 became no. 1258 of the Third Avenue Railway of New York.

The Union Street Railway of New Bedford was the last trolley system in the commonwealth to operate open streetcars in regular revenue service. Car 249, a 13-bench vehicle built by Osgood Bradley in 1910, is at Purchase and Union downtown on August 16, 1936. Opens last ran on September 11, 1938, ten days before the infamous 1938 hurricane caused the Acushnet River to overflow, innundating the Pope's Island carhouse and irreparably damaging the stored open cars' motors.

UNION STREET RAILWAY

TROLLEYS IN NEW BEDFORD

THE UNION STREET RAILWAY of New Bedford resulted from the merger of the New Bedford & Fairhaven and the Acushnet Street Railways on April 30, 1887. The former road had been the city's first, opening in July 1872, while the latter was but three years old. The southeastern Massachusetts port, center of the 19th-century whaling industry, saw its first electric street-car on October 19, 1890, on the Mount Pleasant–Rural Cemetery line.

Electrification proceeded steadily in the early 1890s, but not without opposition. In March 1894 the residents of Fairhaven, on the east side of the Acushnet River from New Bedford, voted in town meeting to instruct selectmen not to permit electric cars in the town. They voiced opposition to the new form of motive power on safety and aesthetic grounds, and expressed fears that the cars would frighten horses. For more than a year the Union had to tow Fairhaven cars as trailers in New Bedford, attaching horses to them at the town line for the rest of their trip. The inconvenience of this practice finally led a May 1895 town meeting to reverse the earlier policy, and the electrification of the line was completed by summer.

Unlike many other urban trolley companies in the state, the Union did not expand outward to any great extent. This conservative policy resulted in a sound fiscal base for the company, which easily survived the financial crunch of the late 1910s that had many of the commonwealth's street railways in bankruptcy; indeed, the USR did not report an operating deficit until 1931, and red ink remained the exception rather than the rule through the end of rail service.

The Union, however, did control two other systems. The Dartmouth & Westport Street Railway, connecting New Bedford and Fall River, came into being as a joint effort between the Union and the Globe Street Railway of Fall River to thwart a rival proposal, the Fall River & New Bedford Street Railway. The D&W, completed in July 1894, helped insure its success by building a major summer resort, Lincoln Park, at the mid-point of its line. By 1898 the USR had eclipsed its partner's interest in the D&W, finally absorbing it in November 1910.

The New Bedford & Onset Street Railway, the pet project of USR President Henry H. Crapo, opened in August 1901, having acquired the East Wareham, Onset Beach & Point Independence three months earlier. That horsecar line had been the successor in 1891 to the Onset Street Railway, opened in 1888.

In June 1906 the New Bedford & Onset acquired the Taunton & Buzzards Bay Street Railway. The T&BB had come into being in February 1905 as the result of the purchase at a receiver's sale of the Middleborough, Wareham & Buzzards Bay, which had been chartered in 1901. With this purchase, the NB&O, which was never merged with the Union, formed a T-shaped system, with the lines north to Middleborough and southeast to Monument Beach branching off the line from New Bedford at Sandusky in Wareham.

The direct line from New Bedford to Middleborough had been constructed by the New Bedford, Middleborough & Brockton Street Railway, chartered in 1900, which became part of the Bay State system. This foreign inroad into Union territory lasted until September 1919, when the Eastern Mass. abandoned the 27-mile route. The USR took over the portion of the line within the city limits at that time.

Shortly after Henry Crapo's death in 1926, the New Bedford & Onset abandoned the line from Sandusky to Middleborough. The remainder of the NB&O was sold in 1927 to a group which replaced rail service with buses on September 30, 1927. As a part of these transactions, the USR acquired the NB&O line from Fairhaven to Mattapoisett.

(An important historical sidelight to the NB&O story came in the autumn of 1915, when the first trackless trolley line in Massachusetts, and one of the pioneer operations in the United States, was instituted to provide a link from Fairhaven to the Mattapoisett line along Sconticut Neck Road.)

The Union remained trolley-oriented into the early 1930s, purchasing a fleet of 12 "Electromobiles" from Osgood Bradley in 1929. The inevitable drop in patronage during the Great Depression, however, led to the start of major conversions to bus operation. Service on the Fall River line west of Lincoln Park went in 1933, with the Mattapoisett run ending in 1935. By the end of 1940 only three routes remained. World War II delayed the final conversions, but on May 3, 1947, trolleys ran their last miles.

Trolleygrams, *Rockwell Collection*

Driver Asa Gray directs the team pulling New Bedford & Fairhaven Street Railway car 1 at the corner of Merrimac and Purchase Sts. in 1874. The bobtail (i.e., single-end) unit was turned at both ends of the route.

Jackson & Sharp, *Carlson Collection*

The Wilmington, Del., firm of Jackson & Sharp furnished many of New Bedford's early electric cars. Combination car 5 was part of the initial equipment acquired by the Dartmouth & Westport Street Railway in 1894. It is here resting on a shop truck at the builder's plant.

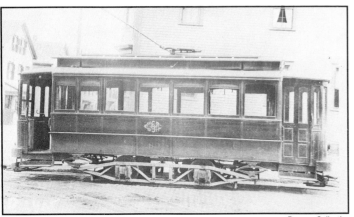

Duncan Collection

In 1895 the Union Street Railway received a lot of 11 single-truck cars with 20-foot 1-inch bodies from Jackson & Sharp. Car 89 of that group survived until 1920.

Trolleygrams, *Hauck Collection*

Around 1900 18 -foot box car 98 is at the end of the Fairhaven line. The motorman is Benson C. Bates, while the conductor is Charles Gooding. The car had been built by Jackson & Sharp in 1895.

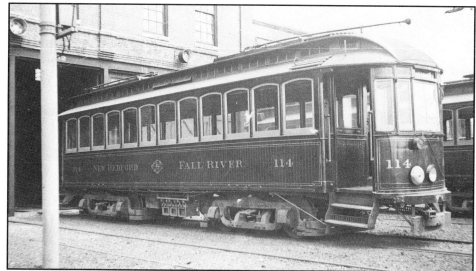

Between 1899 and 1903 a total of eleven 31-foot closed cars were acquired from Jones for use on the Dartmouth & Westport route between New Bedford and Fall River. Car 114 of the earliest group of interurbans is at Pope's Island carhouse in April 1938.

All photos: *Charles A. Duncan*

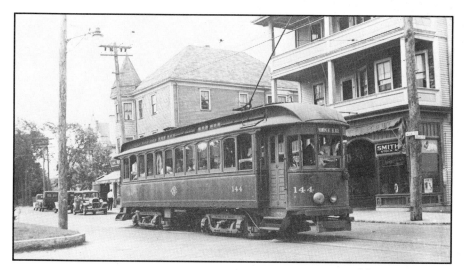

Car 145 (ABOVE) of the 1903 lot is on the Mattapoisett line in downtown New Bedford in April 1935. Three years later, unit 144 (LEFT) was viewed at North Fairhaven.

New Bedford & Onset Street Railway

The New Bedford & Onset commenced operation in 1901 with a dozen 13-bench open cars from Jones. Seen at Wareham, car 150 was transferred to the Union Street Railway in 1906.

Harding Collection

The New Bedford & Onset's cars were similar to those of the Dartmouth & Westport. Charles Hatch and Walter Holbrook pose with NB&O 122, a 1902 Jones product, around 1906. Note the whistle on the roof.

Trolleygrams, Hauck Collection

Rockwell Collection

Rockwell Collection

Middleborough, Wareham & Buzzards Bay 22, at the wharf in Onset, was one of a dozen 12-bench cars built by Wason in 1901. It would become NB&O 222 in 1906.

Car 156, one of the original NB&O units, is on Wareham St. in Middleborough. Most of the NB&O's cars were still on the roster when the road was abandoned on September 30, 1927.

In the fall of 1915 the commonwealth's first trackless trolley operated along Sconticut Neck Road in Fairhaven. The primitive vehicle, which had earlier been used in Merrill, Wisc., meets a car on the NB&O's Mattapoisett line. Unlike later trolley coaches in Boston and Fitchburg, which were legally considered to be streetcars, this unit was registered as a motor vehicle. This pioneering operation ended on December 1, 1915.

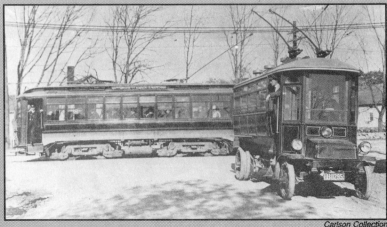

Carlson Collection

All photos: *Charles A. Duncan*

Between 1906 and 1913 the USR received 46 closed cars with 30-foot bodies for local lines in New Bedford and Fairhaven. They became known as "Yellow Belly" cars because of the cream or light yellow concave side panel on an otherwise Pullman green body. All but the last 12 units came from Jones; that lot was built by Osgood Bradley. Car 192 (ABOVE) shows the original width doors which the lowest numbered cars retained throughout their lives. The remaining units were lengthened and equipped with four-leaf folding doors in the mid-1920s for prepayment operation. This arrangement is illustrated on car 235 (ABOVE RIGHT). The 1911 and 1913 deliveries featured five-window fronts. Jones-built 278 and Bradley car 282 from those groups are seen (RIGHT) at Railroad Turnout in Fairhaven in 1936. Two years later cars 211 and 281 (BELOW) meet at Kempton and City Line. Operating on route 2 *Depot* in April 1938 is no. 284 (BELOW RIGHT). This unit was one of the last five active "Yellow Belly" cars, surviving until the end of rail service in 1947.

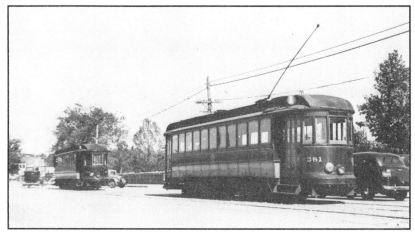

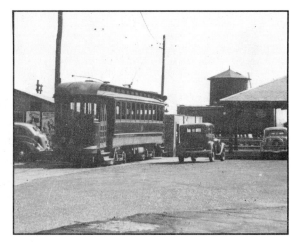

97

The standard open car in New Bedford had 13 benches with three-window bulkheads. In July 1938, the last summer of operation, Jones open 205 of 1908 discharges passengers for Acushnet Park at Fort Rodman.

All photos: *Charles A. Duncan*

One of a dozen cars built by Bradley in 1910, open 239 is seen at Main and Center, Fairhaven, in August 1936, not long before the abandonment of route 10. The circular roof-mounted route numbers were a feature of USR cars, being more visible than the actual destination signs.

In 1901 Wason delivered a group of 12-bench opens to the Middleborough, Wareham & Buzzards Bay Street Railway. Passed on to successor Taunton & Buzzards Bay, they became property of the New Bedford & Onset upon its acquisition of the T&BB in 1906. Six of the 12 cars were later transferred to the Union Street Railway. One of those units is being maneuvered into the Weld St. carhouse in August 1935. Note the umbrella to protect the policeman directing traffic from the elements. The Weld St. barn, adaptively reused for housing, survives in 1989.

In 1910 the USR purchased five 10-bench opens from Jones. The Troy, N.Y., carbuilder was the Union's favorite in the first decade and a half of the century. After 1923 the 10-bench units were the only single-truck cars on the roster. No. 267 rests at Pope's Island in the summer of 1940, shortly before an extensive scrapping program eliminated all open cars from the property.

In 1913 the USR took delivery of two 26-foot arched roof closed cars riding on a radial axle truck. They were later converted to double-truck units, the common end for most radial truck cars. In 1934 both were operating on the 4 *Rivet St.* line. Brill-built 146 (LEFT) is pictured at Rivet and Acushnet Ave., while St. Louis Car product 165 is illustrated in downtown New Bedford.

DON'T FAIL TO VISIT

LINCOLN PARK

On the "Gee Whiz Line"

Midway between New Bedford and Fall River
The People's Pleasure Ground

FREE DANCING
BAND CONCERTS
OPEN AIR THEATRE
COUNTLESS DELIGHTS

Trolley Wayfinder, 1911

Railway-owned Lincoln Park was a popular destination for USR passengers. In June 1937 open 254 changes ends amid track workers. The car was one of 12 vestibuled-front opens outshopped by Jones in 1911.

The last Jones cars delivered to New Bedford were also the Whaling City's longest. The five 33-foot interurban cars were received in 1915, not long before Jones left the carbuilding field. Car 295 poses amid the green grass and flowers of Bridge Park during a 1938 National Railway Historical Society excursion.

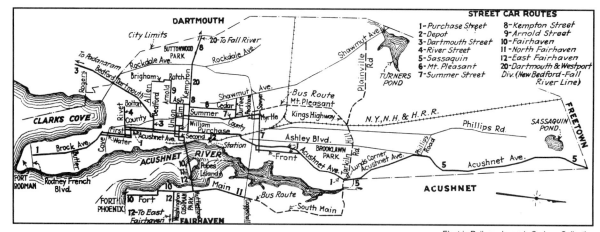

Electric Railway Journal, *Carlson Collection*

This 1929 New Bedford route map shows how much of the system remained rail even at this late date. Major abandonments of car lines would not begin until 1933.

Hauck Collection

In 1920 the USR purchased six second-hand cars from the Second Avenue Railway of New York. Originally built by Brill about 1901 for the Metropolitan Street Railway, they lasted in New Bedford until 1927. Car 455 is at Purchase and William on May 2, 1922.

In 1917 and 1918 Bradley built 18 convertible cars for USR. In April 1940 car 402 passes Fairhaven High School on Huttleston Ave. en route to North Fairhaven. This unit was among the 14 which were equipped with multiple-unit control, although none ever ran in trains.

Charles A. Brown

In 1923 the railway took delivery of six double-truck safety cars from Bradley to replace the ex-Second Avenue equipment. Like other Bradley products in the Whaling City, they were delivered from the Worcester factory under their own power. In July 1938 photographer Charles Duncan found car 501 and open 208 at Fort Rodman.

The dozen "Electromobiles" delivered to New Bedford in 1929 represented the largest of three orders for Osgood Bradley's modern design, which closely resembled Brill's "Master Unit" in appearance. They were assigned to route 1 *Lund's Corner–Fort Rodman*. In May 1939 car 605 heads for the southern terminus of the line.

In June 1940 the operator and a shopman work to replace a broken trolley rope on car 604 outside Weld St. barn. Except for a single PCC car in Boston, the "Electromobiles" were then the most modern street-cars in the commonwealth.

Stanley M. Hauck

Stanley M. Hauck

Car 602 (ABOVE) approaches the loop at Fort Rodman. It was one of seven sold in 1949 to the Queensboro Bridge Railway of New York City. Retaining their original numbers, they crossed the East River between Queens and Manhattan until April 7, 1957, earning the distinction of being the last trolleys to run in the Empire State. Still in New Bedford colors, car 606 (RIGHT) is at the Queens Plaza end of the line in May 1953.

Carlson Collection

101

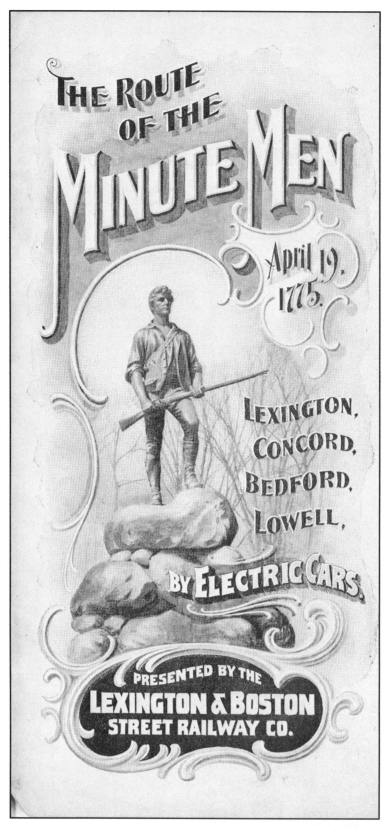

THE ROUTE OF THE MINUTE MEN

April 19, 1775.

Lexington, Concord, Bedford, Lowell, BY ELECTRIC CARS.

PRESENTED BY THE LEXINGTON & BOSTON STREET RAILWAY CO.

LAND OF THE MINUTE MEN

THE MIDDLESEX & BOSTON STREET RAILWAY

THE SMALLEST of the three major street railways in the Greater Boston area, the Middlesex & Boston served the western suburbs. It represented a consolidation of the lines controlled by the Boston Suburban Electric Companies, and achieved its final form on May 9, 1912, when it absorbed the Lexington & Boston Street Railway.

The oldest predecessor of the Middlesex & Boston, the Waltham & Newton, opened on August 31, 1866. That road became part of the Newton Street Railway in 1889. The first electric operation began in Waltham in July 1890.

During the 1890s a group of Newton businessmen established a series of lines in the Newton, Waltham, and Watertown area. These included the Newton & Boston (chartered 1892), the Newtonville & Watertown (1893), the Wellesley & Boston (1895), and the Commonwealth Avenue (1895). The Newtonville & Watertown did not operate under its own name; rather, its tracks were leased jointly to the Newton & Boston and the West End (Boston Elevated).

The Natick Electric came into being in 1891. It became the South Middlesex Street Railway in 1893, the same year it entered Framingham. It then continued to reach westward to Hopkinton. From there, its subsidiary, the Westborough & Hopkinton, built a line to a junction with the Worcester Consolidated at Westborough in 1901.

The Natick & Cochituate Street Railway received its charter in May 1885. Opening two years later, it electrified in 1893. It extended east through Wellesley to Newton Lower Falls in 1896 and south to Needham in 1898. At the same time, it built lines from Cochituate to Wayland and to Saxonville.

The Waltham Street Railway, organized in 1900, was promoted by James Shaw in conjunction with the proposed Boston & Western Street Railway. That latter line, following the Boston Post Road (the present U.S. 20) through Weston and Marlborough, never came into existence because of difficulties in obtaining a franchise in Weston. As a result, Shaw sold the unopened Waltham property to the Newton Street Railway in 1901.

The Newton syndicate organized itself in November 1901 as the Boston Suburban Electric Companies. A year later, the Boston Suburban acquired the Natick & Cochituate. The trust also controlled the Lexington & Boston Street Railway, which opened its first line, from Lexington to Waltham, on April 14, 1900. The Concord & Boston, a subsidiary of the Lexington & Boston, began operation thirteen months later. In November 1902 the L&B extended its route north to Billerica, from where it operated over Lowell Suburban (later Boston & Northern) tracks into Lowell.

While the Commonwealth Avenue and the Wellesley & Boston merged into the Newton in 1903, major consolidations did not take place until after the Boston Suburban purchased the South Middlesex in July 1907. Organizing the Middlesex & Boston to take over the bankrupt property's lines, the trust gradually incorporated its other holdings into that company: the Westborough & Hopkinton and the Natick & Cochituate in 1908, the Newton and the Newton & Boston in 1909, and finally the Lexington & Boston in 1912.

The M&B, while concentrated in the Newton and Waltham area, was a wide-ranging system. It connected with the Bay State at Needham, Billerica, and Woburn; the Boston Elevated at Arlington Heights, Newton (just inside the Brighton line), and Watertown; the Worcester Consolidated at Westborough; the Boston & Worcester in Newton and Framingham; and the Concord, Maynard & Hudson in Concord.

The first abandonments of M&B routes occurred following a 1918 strike, when the Needham–Wellesley and the Lexington–Woburn routes were discontinued. In 1923 the lines from Cochituate to Wayland and Saxonville and from Hopkinton to Westborough were abandoned. The Natick and Lexington divisions were converted to buses in 1925, with the Waltham division following three years later. The "through line" between Newton and Framingham ran for the last time on August 1, 1929. Eight months later, the M&B's final rail line, from Lake St. to Norumbega Park via Commonwealth Ave., was abandoned.

Newton Street Railway horsecar 3 operates as a shuttle car on the wrong track on Moody St., Waltham, on the second day of 1895 during work on the overhead. The car dated from 1882 and had been taken over from the Waltham & Newton Horse Railway.

Jones-built 9-bench open 35 of the Newton Street Railway runs on a tree-lined street in Waltham. This 1897-vintage unit became car 116 in the combined roster of the Boston Suburban Electric Companies.

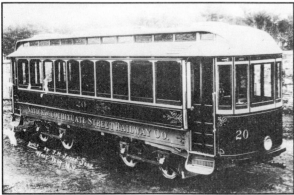

Natick & Cochituate Street Railway 20 poses for its builder's photograph at the West Troy (now Watervliet), N.Y., plant of J. M. Jones' Sons.

Newton & Boston 7 was an 1895 product of the Massachusetts Car Co. of South Ashburnham. This view was taken in front of the Stone estate on Eliot St. in Newton Upper Falls.

The South Middlesex crossed the New Haven Railroad at Charles River Village over this steel viaduct. While this line was abandoned shortly after the South Middlesex was acquired by the Middlesex & Boston, the abutments can still be seen in 1989.

The Commonwealth Avenue Street Railway provided service between Norumbega Park in Auburndale and the Newton-Boston line at Lake St. A large group of ladies crowds around Jones-built 15-bench open no. 28 at the latter location in 1904. The two cars in front of it belong to the Boston Elevated Railway. The structure in the background is St. John's Seminary.

Commonwealth Avenue 21 passes Bullochs Pond at Commonwealth Ave. and Walnut St. near Newton Centre. This 1899 Jones product would later be renumbered 227 in the consolidated roster. The Boston Suburban assigned odd numbers to closed cars and even numbers to its open fleet.

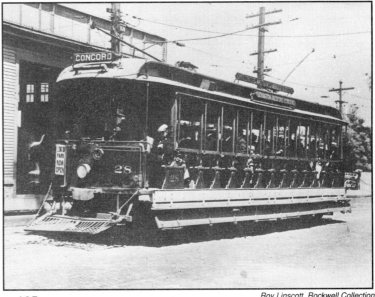

Wason supplied the original rolling stock of the Lexington & Boston in 1900, including 10 with 12 benches such as 18 (ABOVE) on the Woburn line, and 7 with 15 benches. One of the latter group (RIGHT) poses at Arlington Heights in 1906. For the most part, L&B cars kept their numbers after the merger into the Middlesex & Boston in 1912.

Trolley Wayfinder, *1911*

A postcard view of Lexington Park.

Clark Collection

Clark Collection

The Commonwealth Avenue developed Norumbega Park on the Charles River in the Auburndale section of Newton. This was one of the earliest street railway-owned parks in the country. One of the company's two carbarns was built into the lower level of the casino.

Duncan Collection

Four tracks entered the carbarn, while a fifth served the loading platform. All of the 15-bench opens in this 1912 view were originally the property of the Commonwealth Avenue company.

Trolley Wayfinder, *1911*

In addition to drawing patrons to railway-developed parks, the M&B attracted tourists eager to see the many historic sites in Lexington and Concord. Operators of establishments catering to visitors such as the Colonial Inn advertised the trolley as a way to reach them, and the railway provided day tours from Boston. The 12-bench open (ABOVE) was used in excursion service for the average tourist; for special parties the parlor car "Norumbega" (RIGHT) was available.

Clark Collection

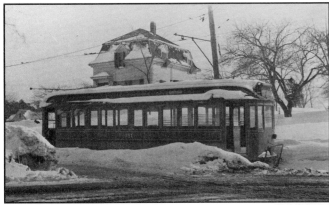

Clark Collection

M&B 361, stranded in the snow at Natick, had been built in 1904 as Natick & Cochituate 28.

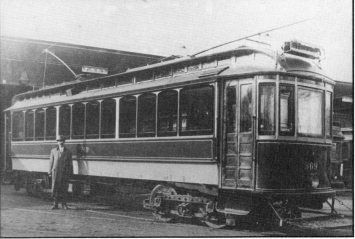

Duncan Collection

The largest closed cars were the 30-foot units built from shorter cars. Company official Pitt Drew poses with spliced car 369 at Auburndale.

Traffic to Hopkinton was heaviest on Patriot's Day, when the M&B transported runners and spectators alike to the starting line of the famed Boston Marathon. One such April 19th is illustrated here. The Marathon still begins at this location, but the trolleys have long since disappeared and the holiday has been shifted to a Monday.

Cummings Collection

Until November 1, 1914, M&B cars operated into Boston's subway via Commonwealth Ave. and Boylston St. In this early 1900s view M&B 119 passes McKim, Mead & White's landmark Boston Public Library in Copley Sq.

Following the cessation of through service, M&B riders changed to Boston Elevated cars at this shelter on Commonwealth Ave. at the Boston-Newton line. The pennant on the trolley pole of Jones 12-bench open 292 was a feature of M&B cars for years. The dark spot on the roof is very likely a defect in the original glass plate negative, exposed by a Boston Elevated photographer in June 1919.

On November 17, 1904, the Lexington & Boston inaugurated service from Sullivan Sq., Charlestown, to Lowell via Arlington, Lexington, Bedford, and Billerica. From Billerica to Lowell the route used the tracks of the Bay State Street Railway. A closed car of that system follows an L&B/M&B 12-bench open in Billerica Center.

When the Cambridge Subway opened in 1912, the Lowell line was rerouted to Harvard Sq. via Massachusetts Ave. Car 234 carries signs for such service as it waits at the North Lexington carhouse in June 1915. A year later, the route was cut back to Arlington Heights to end the last M&B operation over Boston Elevated trackage.

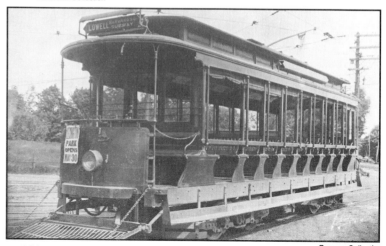

Clark Collection

The most modern cars on the M&B were the six Birneys purchased in 1919. Only two saw service for any length of time, as four were sold to the Connecticut Co. before year's end. Car 505 in Waltham became Connecticut Co. 2222.

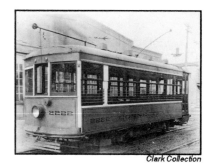

Clark Collection

Charles A. Brown

In the last years of rail service 25-foot car 101 waits at the Lake St. transfer station. As late as 1930 this section of Commonwealth Ave. was predominantly rural in appearance.

The normal method of scrapping streetcars was to set them on fire. Once the flames did their work, the salvageable metal could be collected. Such practices, illustrated here with M&B opens, were acceptable in an era unconcerned with air pollution and other environmental issues.

Charles A. Duncan

The rural nature of much of the New Hampshire Electric Railways system is apparent in this view of Lowell & Pelham Street Railway 25-foot closed car 98 taken on Broadway, Haverhill, between Martin's Siding and Haverhill Junction in August 1905. The 1902 product of the Laconia Car Co. remained on the roster of the Massachusetts Northeastern Street Railway until 1927.

SERVING THE MERRIMACK VALLEY

THE MASSACHUSETTS NORTHEASTERN SYSTEM

THE MASSACHUSETTS NORTHEASTERN STREET RAILWAY came into existence largely as the result of the activity of promoter Wallace D. Lovell. It was the only street railway in Massachusetts to receive legislative permission to consolidate with companies chartered in another state. At its peak, approximately one third of its 130 miles of track were located in New Hampshire.

In 1897 Lovell gained control of the Exeter (N.H.) Street Railway. Under his leadership, that property became the Exeter, Hampton & Amesbury in 1899. At the same time Lovell organized a connecting line in the Bay State, the Amesbury & Hampton Street Railway. His vision of a southeastern New Hampshire-northeastern Massachusetts trolley system also included the Haverhill & Plaistow and two Granite State firms, the Haverhill, Plaistow & Newton and the Seabrook & Hampton Beach.

In the summer of 1901 Lovell gained control of three lines originally promoted by Charles E. Barnes of Malden: the Hudson, Pelham & Salem Electric in New Hampshire and the Haverhill & Southern New Hampshire and the Lawrence & Methuen in Massachusetts. To this group, Lovell added the Lowell & Pelham. These various routes, connecting Haverhill with Lawrence, Lowell, and Nashua, opened in 1902.

The bondholders in Lovell's various railway enterprises organized the New Hampshire Traction Co. in late 1901 to take over the properties from the financially-strapped promoter. Initially, the holding company grouped the lines around the Exeter, Hampton & Amesbury and the Hudson, Pelham & Salem Electric. Both of these firms, however, went into receivership in 1904. The leases of companies to the EH&A were abrogated, and that line was dumped by the holding company, which itself underwent a reorganization in 1905. It emerged as the New Hampshire Electric Railways. The HP&SE remained under its control, becoming the Hudson, Pelham & Salem in 1907.

In that same year Newburyport promoter E. P. Shaw transferred his railway holdings to the Merrimac Valley Electric Company. Those two roads were the Citizens' Electric Street Railway and the Haverhill & Amesbury. The former firm had taken over the property of the Newburyport & Amesbury Horse Railroad at a receiver's sale in 1899. A year later it absorbed the Plum Island Electric Street Railway, started in 1897 to link Newburyport with the Parker River area. The Newburyport & Amesbury, chartered in 1864, opened its first line in July 1873 and began electric service in October 1889. Shaw's other property, the Haverhill & Amesbury, had commenced operation in October 1892, shortly after it had acquired the Black Rocks & Salisbury Beach, a seasonal line incorporated in 1884 which used first horsecars and then steam dummies.

In 1909 Shaw sold the Haverhill & Amesbury to the New Hampshire Electric Railways. Two years later, the Citizens' Electric was conveyed as well. At the same time, both states were approached for permission to consolidate the various firms into a single entity. In preparation for this action, the Haverhill & Southern New Hampshire changed its name to the Massachusetts Northeastern Street Railway (MNE) on June 26, 1912. Nine months later it absorbed the nine other companies. (The New Hampshire Electric Railways' other property, the Dover, Somersworth & Rochester, remained independent.)

The MNE served all of the communities on the north shore of the Merrimack River in Massachusetts and their neighbors across the state line. It connected with the Bay State at Newburyport, Haverhill, Lawrence, Lowell, and Nashua. It also met the Exeter, Hampton & Amesbury and the Portsmouth Electric Railway at Hampton Beach, N.H.

Because a large portion of the MNE's business was seasonal, carrying passengers to the various resorts served by it, the company was hard hit by automobile competition in the 1920s. In 1923 the route from Seabrook to Newton, N.H., through Amesbury and from Lowell to Pelham, N.H., went, followed in 1924 by service from Salem, N.H., to Nashua. Five years later the lines to Salem and Canobie Lake Park were discontinued. Now in receivership, the MNE converted its remaining lines to buses between August 27 and September 7, 1930.

A team of three horses pulls an open car of the Newburyport & Amesbury Horse Railroad across the Chain Bridge over the Merrimack River between Newburyport and Deer Island, Amesbury. Until E. P. Shaw purchased its holdings in 1886, the town of Newburyport was the largest stockholder in the N&A. Cables replaced the distinctive chains on this span in 1910.

Nowell Collection

Nowell Collection

The Haverhill & Amesbury operated a steam dummy line from Salisbury Beach north to the state line from 1899 to 1902. When the line was electrified, 15-bench open trailer 32 was rebuilt as a motor car.

Cummings Collection

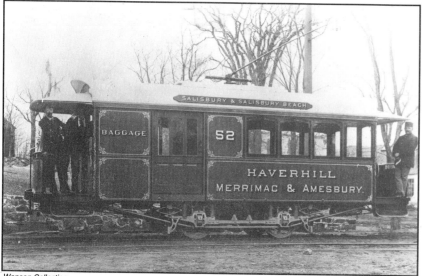

Another resort area served by trolleys was Plum Island. Newburyport-built 12-bench open 90 of the Citizens' Electric Street Railway poses at Marston's Pavilion. The conductor at the right is Cyrus "Uncle Cy" Adams.

Haverhill & Amesbury combination car 52 had a 20-foot body and was built by the Briggs Carriage Co. of Amesbury. Ironically, the owner of the H&A was Edward P. Shaw, a principal in the Newburyport Car Co.

Although it at one time controlled by lease many of the lines which would become the Mass. Northeastern, the Exeter, Hampton & Amesbury remained an independent line after emerging from receivership in 1908. Car 20 was a convertible built by Briggs in 1899 under license from the Duplex Car Co. of New York. The owners of the Briggs firm were among the initial stockholders in the EH&A's Massachusetts connection, the Amesbury & Hampton.

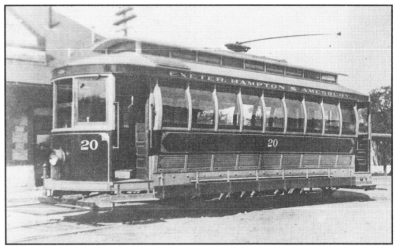

George Allen, Nowell Collection

Cummings Collection

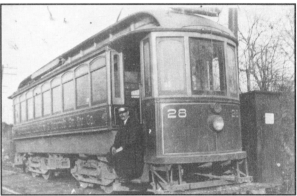

Nowell Collection

Painted for the Haverhill, Plaistow & Newton, 25-foot closed car 28 at one time belonged to the Portsmouth & Exeter, an ill-fated line which was abandoned by the New Hampshire Electric Railways in 1912.

Between 1901 and 1903 the New Hampshire Traction Co. purchased 53 opens with 14 benches from Laconia for its trolley properties. Car 83 at Kenoza Lake in Haverhill was originally assigned to the Haverhill, Plaistow & Newton and lasted until 1929.

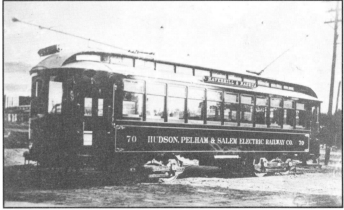

Car 70 was among the thirteen 30-foot cars built by Laconia in 1902 for the Haverhill–Nashua and the Haverhill–Lawrence service. It was sold to Reading, Pa., in 1929, where it became car 148.

Nowell Collection

When it took over the Citizens' Electric in 1911, the New Hampshire Electric Railways transferred cars to the Port City to replace older vehicles. The two cars in Market Sq., Newburyport, are 110, a 21-foot car from the Dover, Somersworth & Rochester, and 25-foot unit 36 from the Portsmouth & Exeter. Both remained as Northeastern cars until scrapped in 1927.

Nowell Collection

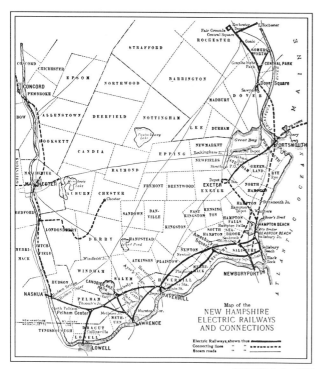

Trolley Wayfinder, 1911

Wonson Collection

Open 163 and another MNE car unload at the bandstand at Hampton Beach, N.H., in an era before private automobiles clogged access to the seashore and took away the trolley line's business.

A major portion of the Mass. Northeastern's business was transporting people from the textile cities of the Merrimack Valley to various shore and other resort areas. Two open cars (RIGHT) are at Salisbury Beach in this 1910 photograph. At this time the company was changing from the maroon-and-cream livery seen on 169 to the chrome yellow paint found on 175.

Cummings Collection

The principal resort on the Northeastern system was Canobie Lake Park in Salem, N.H. This view shows Laconia-built open 143 at the recreation area. Although the railway has long since been abandoned, the park is still in operation in 1989.

Nowell Collection

To replace cars lost in a 1916 Merrimac carhouse fire, the MNE ordered a dozen semi-convertibles from Laconia which were near duplicates of experimental car 4200 of the Bay State Street Railway. Car 144 poses at the Salem, N.H., carhouse in November 1916, shortly after its trip by railroad flatcar from the northern New Hampshire factory. World events of the day led to this class becoming known as "U-boats."

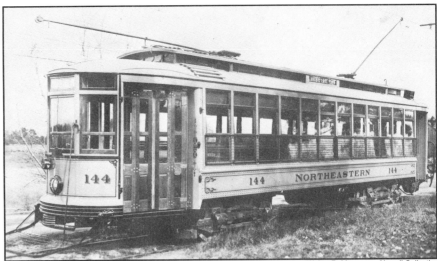

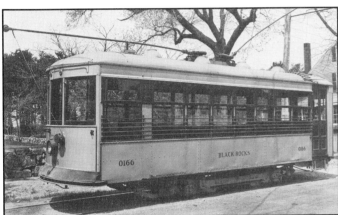

In 1921 Wason delivered six Birneys to the MNE, the first one-man cars on the system. After the Northeastern ceased operations the units were sold to the Biddeford & Saco Railroad of Biddeford, Me.

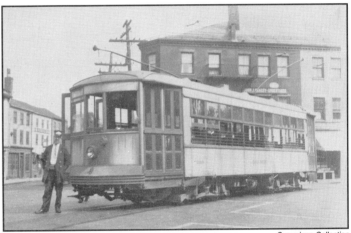

Three years later the Springfield carbuilder supplied five double-truck lightweights which, like the Birneys, bore names in addition to numbers. Motorman James C. Delano stands in front of the "Chain Bridge" in Newburyport. The "Sun Parlors," so-called because of their large windows, subsequently served the Virginia Electric & Power Co. in Richmond, Va.

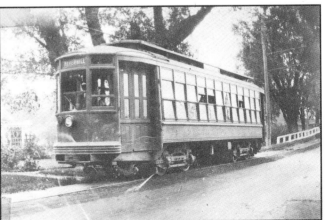

Lighweight 0176, the "Deer Island," (LEFT) enters Market Sq., Amesbury, on the last day of the Newburyport–Amesbury line. "U-boat" 136 (RIGHT) was captured for posterity on Elm St., Amesbury, on September 6, 1930, the next-to-the-last day of rail service on the MNE.

The Greenfield & Montague Transportation Area was the publicly-owned successor in part to the Connecticut Valley Street Railway, one of the three lines comprising the Massachusetts Consolidated Railways. In December 1926 the property ordered two lightweight cars from Wason. In addition to numbers, the units carried Indian names. The "Mohawk" is in downtown Greenfield in August 1929. Following abandonment of rail service, the lightweights were sold to the Cape Breton Tramways of Sydney, Nova Scotia.

NORTHERN MASS. & THE CONNECTICUT VALLEY

THE MASSACHUSETTS CONSOLIDATED RAILWAYS

FORMED IN NOVEMBER 1911, the Massachusetts Northern Railways changed its name to the Massachusetts Consolidated Railways on April 30, 1913, probably to avoid confusion with the newly-renamed Northern Massachusetts Street Railway. A voluntary trust, the Mass. Consolidated consisted of three properties across the north central part of the state—the Concord, Maynard & Hudson, the Northern Massachusetts, and the Connecticut Valley Street Railways. Despite the name, the lines did not connect with each other. A fourth property, the Millers River Street Railway, which would have linked the Northern Mass. and the Connecticut Valley, was never constructed.

ESTABLISHED IN 1899 to construct a line to connect its namesake towns, the Concord, Maynard & Hudson opened on August 1, 1901. Six months later it absorbed the Concord & Clinton Street Railway. While originally a competitive line from Maynard to Concord via Acton, it had come under common ownership with the CM&H before work began. Thus, it built the segment of the route in Concord, connecting with the CM&H at the Acton line.

Chartered in 1900, the Lowell, Acton & Maynard Street Railway never achieved its proposed route from Lowell to Framingham. Only the segments from Maynard to South Acton (opened 1903) and from South Acton to West Acton (opened 1909) were built. Forming a branch of the CM&H, it merged with it on August 26, 1911.

The Concord, Maynard & Hudson came under the control of the Massachusetts Northern Railways in 1912. Like the other lines owned by the trust, the CM&H went into receivership on December 21, 1921. Local interest in reviving the line under public auspices came to naught, and it was abandoned on January 16, 1923.

THE NORTHERN MASSACHUSETTS came into being in 1913 through a change in name by the Athol & Orange Street Railway. The A&O had earlier absorbed the Templeton and the Gardner, Westminster & Fitchburg Street Railways. The three lines formed an end-to-end system between Athol and Fitchburg, with a major branch running north from East Templeton to Winchendon.

The oldest of the properties, the Gardner, Westminster & Fitchburg, had originated in April 1890 as the Gardner Street Railway. Reorganized as the Gardner Electric in the mid-1890s,

it became the GW&F at the turn of the century. The Athol & Orange opened in 1895, with the Templeton road being incorporated a year later.

The Northern Mass. exemplified one of the problems encountered in street railway mergers: it saddled the profitable Athol & Orange with two unprofitable lines. The solution which emerged from the Northern Mass. bankruptcy was the creation of the Atol & Orange Transportation Area to continue the 6.78-mile segment in Athol and abandonment on March 31, 1924, of the remainder of the 45-mile system. One of two publicly-owned transportation areas created under a 1920 state law, the Athol & Orange continued trolley service into the early 1930s. (Also emerging from the Northern Mass. was the Gardner & Templeton, which lasted only until August 1926.)

THE NORTHAMPTON & AMHERST STREET RAILWAY was organized in September 1897 by street railway promoter F. S. Coolidge of Fitchburg. The road opened in January 1900. The delay in construction had been caused both by the opposition of the Amherst & Sunderland Street Railway (opened in 1897 and absorbed by the Holyoke Street Railway five years later) to the granting of a franchise to the N&A in Amherst and the necessity of seeking legislative approval for the construction of a bridge across the Connecticut River. Indeed, for a year after the line's opening passengers had to transfer to a horse-drawn bus for the journey across the river pending completion of the railway bridge. A second line, reaching north to Laurel Park and Hatfield, opened in July 1900.

Trolleys came to Greenfield on June 22, 1895, with the opening of the Greenfield & Turners Falls Street Railway. Five years later the Greenfield & Deerfield was formed, becoming part of the Greenfield, Deerfield & Northampton three years later. Both the G&TF and the GD&N became part of the Northampton & Amherst in March 1905. Two months later the N&A changed its name to the Connecticut Valley Street Railway.

The dissolution of the Mass. Consolidated's subsidiaries had the least effect on the Connecticut Valley. The segments from Northampton to North Hatfield and to Amherst were sold to the Northampton Street Railway, while the line between Greenfield and Montague was taken over by the Greenfield & Montague Transportation Area. The G&MTA survived for a decade as a streetcar operator, finally converting the last of its 8.7 miles of rails to buses on July 7, 1934.

The Concord, Maynard & Hudson opened with a roster consisting of six 25-foot closed cars and an equal number of 12-bench opens. One of the former units (LEFT) is at the end of the South Acton branch around 1903 or 1904 while open no. 11 (RIGHT) crosses the Sudbury River bridge in Concord en route to Hudson.

Hudson was a major junction point between three street railways—the Concord, Maynard & Hudson, the Worcester Consolidated, and the Boston & Worcester. WCSR 303 can barely be seen behind CM&H open 13 in this circa 1902 Main St. view. Renumbered 205 after 1912, the CM&H unit was destroyed in the Maynard carhouse fire of January 25, 1918.

Four of the original closed cars were also destroyed in the Maynard carhouse blaze. To replace them, the CM&H purchased four 30-foot cars from Kuhlman, one of which operates in Concord.

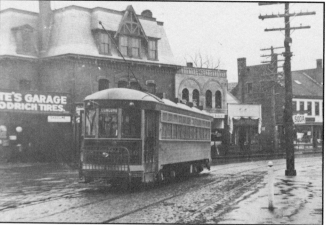

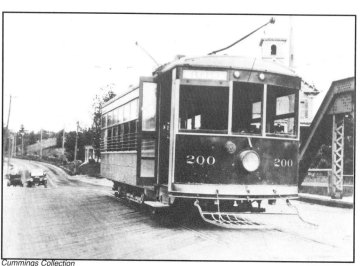

The last car acquired by the CM&H was Birney 200, outshopped by the American Car Co. of St. Louis in 1919. Here crossing the Boston & Maine at South Acton, the single-truck unit was sold to the Bangor (Me.) Street Railway following the 1923 abandonment of the system.

Gardner was a major center of the furniture industry in the commonwealth. In this pre-1908 postcard view a 9-bench open of the Gardner, Westminster & Fitchburg passes the giant chair that has been a local landmark for many decades.

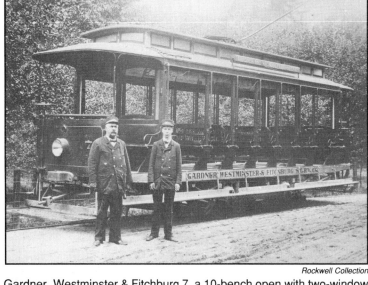

Gardner, Westminster & Fitchburg 7, a 10-bench open with two-window bulkheads, poses at Wachusett Park in 1904. The crew consists of motorman George Smith and conductor Oral Plumb.

Templeton Street Railway 3 was a combination passenger and express car. The road merged into the Athol & Orange on New Year's Day of 1913.

Single-truck car 16 and a double-truck unit of the Athol & Orange meet. The Athol & Orange was the company around which the Northern Mass. was built.

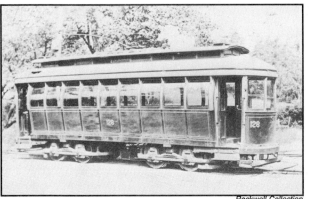

The Mass. Consolidated renumbered all of its subsidiary roads' cars into a common roster. Northern Mass. units occupied the 100 series, along with those of the Connecticut Valley. Duplex-type convertible 128 of the Northern Mass. had been the property of the Templeton Street Railway.

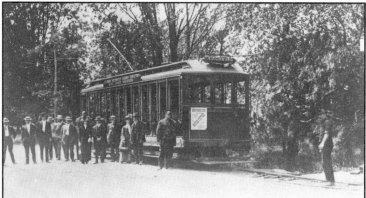

While the front sign on Northern Mass. cars could be changed to show the destination of the unit, the fixed side sign showed all major points that the railway served. The open at Wachusett Park is no. 101.

The Athol & Orange Transportation Area received the best equipment of the Northern Mass. in 1924. The municipally-owned line also acquired former CM&H car 204, spotted on the carhouse lead ahead of ex-Northern Mass. 162.

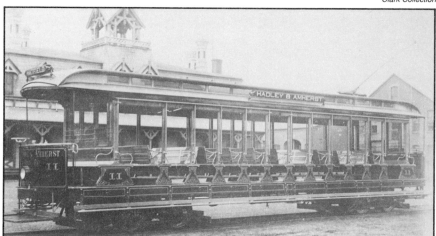

The Northampton & Amherst was the core system for the Connecticut Valley consolidation. N&A 15-bench open 11 poses for the builder's photographer at the Wason plant in Springfield.

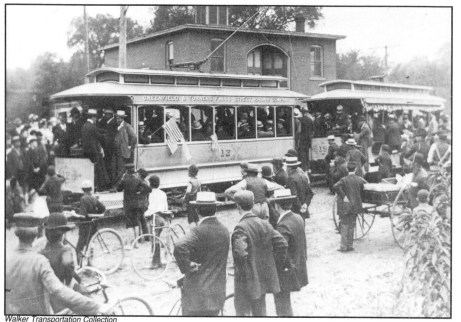

Greenfield & Turners Falls Street Railway 12 and 15 are filled with passengers on the opening day of the line, June 22, 1895. Note the large number of bicycles among the spectators. The construction of the line had taken only 64 days.

Streetcars dominate this view of downtown Greenfield taken about 1903 or 1904. The single-truck cars are the property of the Greenfield & Turners Falls, while double-truck unit 6 belonged to the Greenfield, Deerfield & Northampton Street Railway. The watering trough to the right is a piece of street furniture which has gone the way of the trolleys.

Bound for Northampton is 14-bench vestibule-front open 33. The Mass. Consolidated renumbered this car 133.

Conductor Mike Varilly and motorman Jake Haigis pose with car 114 at Millers Falls around 1912.

Connecticut Valley Street Ry.

Through the heart of the far famed Connecticut Valley

The 1927 Wason lightweights of the Greenfield & Montague Transportation Area were named the "Mohawk" and the "Mohican" while the 1929 cars were the "Picomegan" and "Pocumtuck." The near car in this view is headed west on Main St. in Greenfield while the car behind is waiting to head south toward Deerfield St.

Herbert Ashworth, Clark Collection

The Shelburne Falls & Colrain Street Railway opened on November 3, 1896, connecting its two namesake communities. Barely profitable over its first two decades, the line had heavy losses for all but two years after 1917, and service ended in April 1927. The railway is best remembered for this 400-foot concrete bridge across the Deerfield River, constructed in 1909 to provide a link between the railway and the Boston & Maine Railroad at Buckland, which became the famed "Bridge of Flowers." Car 11, a former horsecar purchased for $150 from the West End Street Railway of Boston in July 1896, heads from Buckland into Shelburne Falls around 1910. Snowplow 24 can be seen on a siding at the end of the span.

ACROSS THE COMMONWEALTH

THE SMALLER TROLLEY SYSTEMS

IN 1916 seven major railway systems accounted for nearly 83 percent of the street railway trackage in Massachusetts and carried 90 percent of the revenue passengers. Some 24 smaller lines also served the commonwealth. These ranged in size from the Point Shirley Street Railway, with 1.2 miles of track, to the Holyoke Street Railway, with 72.3 miles and a ridership approaching 15 million passengers.

This chapter covers these smaller properties in alphabetical order. In a survey of this nature, it is not possible to provide a detailed history of each company outside of the information presented in the captions; however, a few more important properties will be discussed here.

NATIONWIDE, the Boston engineering and utilities management firm of Stone & Webster played a major role in the traction scene, operating systems in cities such as Dallas and Seattle. Most of its properties, however, were small. Thus, one of its engineers, Charles O. Birney, developed the single-truck, one-man safety car for use on lightly-patronized routes.

Stone & Webster held but 73 miles of railways in its home state, concentrated in southeastern Massachusetts. These included the Blue Hill, the Brockton & Plymouth, the Norfolk & Bristol, and the Norwood, Canton & Sharon Street Railways. All were in receivership by the late 1910s. Only the Brockton & Plymouth survived into the 1920s to operate Birneys, although many of those ordered for it were diverted to other Stone & Webster properties. Reorganized as the Plymouth & Brockton Street Railway in 1922, it ended trolley service on June 28, 1928, but survives in 1989 as an operator of commuter bus service between Boston and the South Shore.

THE BOSTON & WORCESTER STREET RAILWAY was the only Massachusetts line which came close to resembling the standard Midwest interurban. The B&W, promoted by James F. Shaw, began operation from Boston to Framingham on May 5, 1903. The full 40.41-mile route from Park Sq., Boston, to City Hall, Worcester, opened two months later.

In addition to the main line, the Boston & Worcester operated local lines in Marlborough and Framingham. These operations were acquired in 1903 and 1904 with the Framingham Union, the Framingham, Southborough & Marlborough, and the Marlborough & Framingham (successor to the Marlborough) Street Railways.

The B&W went into receivership in 1925, emerging in December 1927 as the Boston, Worcester & New York Street Railway. Between 1925 and 1928 all of the system's branches

and Marlborough local services were converted to buses. The main line west of Framingham Center ceased operation in January 1931. All rail service ended eighteen months later.

THE FITCHBURG & LEOMINSTER STREET RAILWAY came into being on April 1, 1892, through the merger of the Fitchburg Street Railway and the Leominster Street Railway. The former had opened as a horsecar line on July 3, 1886, while the latter had been chartered just a year earlier and had not yet been put into service. Electric operation commenced on June 23, 1892.

In 1905 the F&L absorbed the Leominster, Shirley & Ayer. At its peak, the company operated some 41 miles of track and made connections with the Lowell & Fitchburg at Ayer, the Northern Massachusetts at Fitchburg, and the Worcester Consolidated at both Fitchburg and Leominster. (The WCSR had its own parallel route between the two cities, inherited from the former Fitchburg & Suburban.)

By the early 1930s only six local routes remained, and on May 7, 1932, the last streetcars ran on the F&L. But the company had not abandoned electric transit, for three days later it became the first street railway in the commonwealth and the 27th in the country to institute trackless trolleys. The coaches served the F&L for a little over 14 years, the poles finally coming down on July 1, 1946.

TWO RAILWAYS bridged the gap in the Connecticut River Valley between the holdings of the New Haven in Springfield and those of the Massachusetts Consolidated at Deerfield and Greenfield. The older of these lines had opened as the Northampton & Williamsburgh Railroad in October 1866, the first horsecar company in western Massachusetts. Becoming the Northampton Street Railway in 1873, it electrified its lines two decades later.

The Holyoke Street Railway commenced service on September 24, 1884, and ran its first electric car on August 2, 1891. In 1902 it absorbed the Hampshire and the Amherst & Sunderland Street Railways. The former had been incorporated in 1902, while the latter dated from 1896. The HSR also controlled by lease the Mount Tom Railroad, chartered in 1896.

In 1912 the HSR and the NSR came under common control. While run as an entity, with many through routes and joint operation with its neighboring railways to the north and south, the two firms were never consolidated or managed through a holding company. Both railways operated into the 1930s, with Northampton quitting on December 25, 1933, while Holyoke hung on until September 7, 1937.

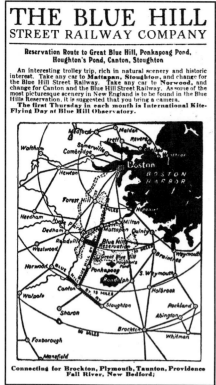

THE BLUE HILL
STREET RAILWAY COMPANY

Reservation Route to Great Blue Hill, Ponkapoag Pond, Houghton's Pond, Canton, Stoughton

An interesting trolley trip, rich in natural scenery and historic interest. Take any car to **Mattapan, Stoughton,** and change for the Blue Hill Street Railway. Take any car to **Norwood,** and change for Canton and the Blue Hill Street Railway. As some of the most picturesque scenery in New England is to be found in the Blue Hills Reservation, it is suggested that you bring a camera.

The first Thursday in each month is International Kite-Flying Day at Blue Hill Observatory.

Connecting for Brockton, Plymouth, Taunton, Providence Fall River, New Bedford)

Trolley Wayfinder, 1911

Walker Transportation Collection

Promoted by Stone & Webster, the Blue Hill Street Railway opened its first segment on November 3, 1899, using 16-foot closed cars purchased from the Boston Elevated. Car 12, on Washington St., Canton, was lost when fire destroyed the Canton Junction carhouse on February 21, 1909.

Walker Transportation Collection

Governor John Bates was among the dignitaries carried on the first trip over the entire Blue Hill route from Stoughton to Mattapan Sq. via Canton on August 14, 1903. The new Stephenson 12-bench opens such as car 65 on the Neponset River bridge at Mattapan were full on that occasion.

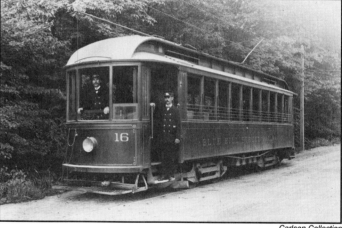

Carlson Collection

Car 16 was one of four Laconia 28-foot semi-convertibles acquired in 1900. Motorman James Dugan and conductor Avery Briggs pose with it on side-of-the-road trackage near the Milton-Canton town line.

Stone & Webster sold the Blue Hill property to Michael A. Cavanaugh in 1917. He was equally unsuccessful at making the line profitable, and in April 1919 it went into receivership. The end came on February 5, 1920, when a blizzard prevented coal from being delivered to the power station and the cars became stranded where they were when the generators stopped. A shoveler assists one of the line's two nose plows to extricate a 21-foot semi-convertible from the snow. The semi-convertibles had been purchased from Wason to replace cars lost in the 1909 carhouse fire.

Duncan Collection

124

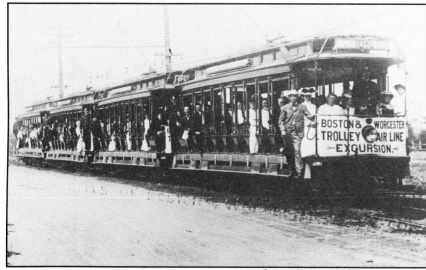

Among the original cars of the Boston & Worcester Street Railway were ten 14-bench opens built by Newburyport. Car 96 of that lot leads this excursion, destination unknown. It was natural that the initial equipment orders should go to Newburyport, since the B&W had been promoted by James F. Shaw, a principal in the carbuilding firm.

Boston & Worcester St. Ry., Wonson Collection

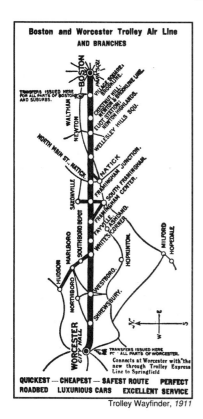

Trolley Wayfinder, 1911

Boston Elevated Railway

In July 1906 Brill delivered six semi-convertibles similar in design to Boston's Type 2 cars. At 53-feet overall length, the "Battleships" were possibly the longest non-articulated cars built for a New England property. They were scrapped in 1928.

Closed car 101 on the Boston run connects with 12-bench open 84, assigned to the Hudson line, at Framingham.

Wonson Collection

Nine-bench open 24, built by the short-lived Morse Car Co. of Millbury, Mass., operates on the Marlborough crosstown line in 1908.

Rockwell Collection

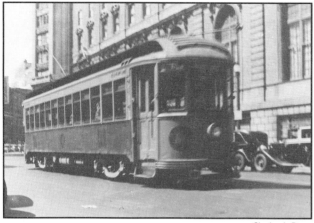

Bradley-built car 133 of 1910 (RIGHT) is at the corner of Union Ave., Framingham Center, in January 1931, while no. 147 (ABOVE) is on Columbus Ave., Boston, shortly before the June 10, 1932, abandonment of the remaining rail service on the "Trolley Air Line."

Brockton & Plymouth Street Railway

STONE & WEBSTER promoted the Brockton & Plymouth and the Pembroke Street Railways at the turn of the century to link Brockton and Plymouth on a route passing through Whitman, Hanson, Pembroke, and Kingston. Opened in July 1900, the two lines and the Plymouth & Kingston (inaugurated in June 1889) were consolidated in November as the Brockton & Plymouth.

The B&P went into receivership in 1919, emerging three years later as the Plymouth & Brockton. The route west of Kingston was abandoned at the end of the 1925 summer season; the line to Plymouth struggled on for three more years.

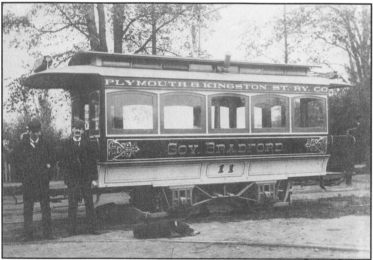

The Plymouth & Kingston's early cars bore names of the Pilgrim Fathers. The "Governor Bradford" honored the second head and chief chronicler of the Plymouth Colony.

In 1900 New Hampshire's Laconia Car Co. outshopped 30-foot closed car 32. The 15-bench open behind it was purchased for the proposed but never built Holbrook & Weymouth Street Railway and added to the Plymouth & Kingston roster in 1899.

One of the chief traffic generators on the line was Mayflower Grove in Bryantville. Car 33 was a 12-bench unit built by Laconia in 1900 as part of the original equipment of the B&P.

126

George E. Lewis, Rockwell Collection

The derailment of one of the B&P's two nose plows in the Bryantville section of Hanson resulted in this gathering of equipment. First in line is single-truck closed car 14, acquired second-hand from New Orleans, La., in 1902. It had been built in 1893 by St. Louis Car for the New Orleans & Carrollton Railroad's first electric line, the still-operating St. Charles route. Following it is freight car 101 and what appears to be a 30-foot passenger unit.

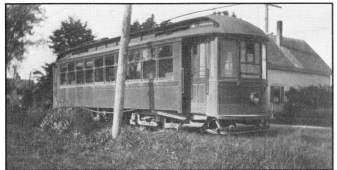

Rockwell Collection

In October 1920 noted Washington-area railfan LeRoy O. King, Sr., snapped this view of Laconia-built car 30.

Rockwell Collection

On occasion, the B&P borrowed equipment from its sister Stone & Webster line, the Blue Hill. Blue Hill 18, passing through Bryantville, was permanently transferred to the Brockton & Plymouth in 1903.

The most modern car on the Plymouth & Brockton was Brill lightweight 400, delivered in 1922. With the abandonment of the P&B in 1928, car 400 was sold to Maine's Waterville, Fairfield & Oakland Street Railway and renumbered 60. Signed for Waterville in 1935, it remained in service until the WF&O ended trolley operation on October 10, 1937.

Rockwell Collection

Conway Electric Street Railway

WHILE the New Haven Railroad owned over 700 miles of street railway in Massachusetts, the Boston & Maine had but 6.5 miles—the Conway Electric Street Railway. Opened on April 1, 1895, the system had been promoted by local business interests in an attempt to reverse losses of population and industry because of the town being bypassed by steam railroad lines. For the decade from 1908 to 1919, the B&M owned the line. Service continued under local ownership until the spring of 1921.

Clark Collection

In 1916 the system reported ownership of three passenger cars—one open, possibly car 5, and two combines.

Wason-built 1 was the original vehicle on the system. The number of combines indicates the importance that the carriage of milk and freight played in the financial affairs of the property.

Cummings Collection

Duncan Collection

The Norfolk Western Street Railway opened in 1899 to connect Medfield with Dedham Sq. An open car loads on High St., Dedham. The Dedham Institution for Savings forms the backdrop in this photograph taken just before the turn of the century.

Walker Transportation Collection

The Dedham & Franklin Street Railway succeeded the Norfolk Western in 1904. Closed car 11 and convertible 1 are entering the Westwood carhouse.

In June 1914 the Dedham & Franklin was sold at a receiver's sale to the Medway & Dedham. The Milford & Uxbridge Street Railway operated that line under lease until abandonment in November 1924. In 1919 the M&D purchased four Birneys from Wason, an unusual development for a line leased to another. Car 101 is snowbound on the line amid debris from a fallen tree.

Cummings Collection

East Taunton Street Railway

THE EAST TAUNTON STREET RAILWAY opened its line from Taunton to East Taunton on December 23, 1898. During the following year it was extended to Middleborough. While the Middleborough service was discontinued in May 1929, the railway operated trolleys in Taunton until August 13, 1932, little more than a month after the Eastern Mass. had substituted buses on its local routes.

In 1903 the railway acquired two 13-bench opens from Laconia. One of those units here carries a capacity crowd.

Taunton was one of the few smaller cities in the state to have as many as three separate street railways operating within its limits as late as the mid-1920s. Those firms were the Eastern Mass., the Norton, Taunton & Attleborough, and the East Taunton. The crew of East Taunton 4 pose with their car in front of City Hall around 1899.

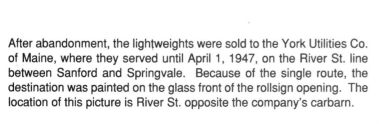

In 1926 the East Taunton purchased two lightweight cars from Wason. Car 12 is passing Taunton Green in this September 1928 view. The car is now preserved at the Seashore Trolley Museum.

After abandonment, the lightweights were sold to the York Utilities Co. of Maine, where they served until April 1, 1947, on the River St. line between Sanford and Springvale. Because of the single route, the destination was painted on the glass front of the rollsign opening. The location of this picture is River St. opposite the company's carbarn.

Rotograph Co., Rockwell Collection

Clark Collection

The Fitchburg & Leominster Street Railway provided trolley service in Fitchburg, Leominster, Lancaster, Lunenburg, Shirley, Harvard, and Ayer. Three key points on the system were Depot Sq., Fitchburg (ABOVE), Monument Sq., Leominster (ABOVE RIGHT), and Whalom Park, Lunenburg (RIGHT), a company-owned amusement center and summer theater. These postcard views date from the middle of the first decade of the century.

Rotograph Co., Clark Collection

FITCHBURG & LEOMINSTER Street Railway Co.

Rockwell Collection

Jones-built 19 was part of a large fleet of 9-bench open cars owned by the Fitchburg & Leominster.

Carlson Collection

Part of the preparation for departure from Monument Sq. to Whalom Park was extending the fender. Car 14, a 13-bench open built by Wason in 1905, is preserved at the Illinois Railway Museum at Union, Ill.

The F&L operated through service with the Athol & Orange (later Northern Mass.). In this January 1912 view, A&O line car 15 has come to the rescue of F&L 51, which derailed at the foot of Ladder Hill in Templeton.

In 1910 Wason delivered a pair of 31-foot 10-inch semi-convertibles to the F&L, numbered 4 and 34 (BELOW). The non-sequential numbers were assigned to fill gaps in the roster caused by the scrapping of earlier cars.

Rockwell Collection

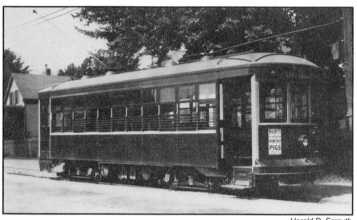

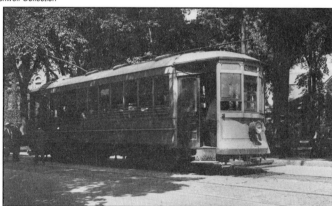

Harold D. Forsyth

Harold D. Forsyth

Between 1926 and 1928 the F&L acquired 10 lightweight cars from Wason. The first of the lot (ABOVE) is at the end of the Cleghorn line in the summer of 1930. Like most modern cars in Massachusetts, they were sold for use elsewhere after abandonment. In this case, the purchaser was the Bristol Traction Co. of Connecticut. In June 1935 Bristol Traction 42 (RIGHT) was caught by photographer William Watts near Bristol.

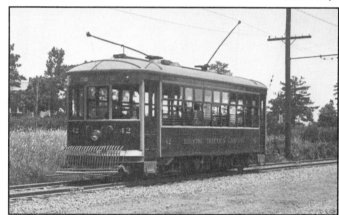

On May 10, 1932, three days after the end of rail operation, electric transit returned to the F&L in the form of trackless trolleys. The fleet of seven Brill T-40 coaches served the two north central Massachusetts communities until June 30, 1946. Coach 105 is at Monument Sq., Leominster. After closure of the F&L system, the vehicles were sold to Des Moines, Iowa, where they served until 1953.

William Quance

Holyoke Street Railway

Holyoke Street Railway horsecar 1 is at the South Hadley Falls stable and carbarn in the 1880s. The front dasher shows a destination of "Conn. River Depot," while the side letterboard reads "Main, Canal, and Bridge Sts."

Signed for Elmwood, 20-foot closed car 36 was part of a group of 12 Wason products occupying even numbers from 32 to 54 on the roster.

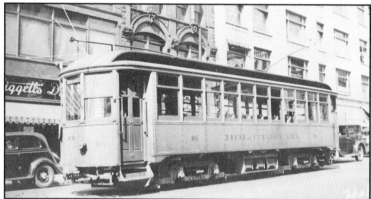

Car 86 passes City Hall, Holyoke in September 1935. The sign over the center window is not the destination but instructions to passengers to "Pay [as you] Enter."

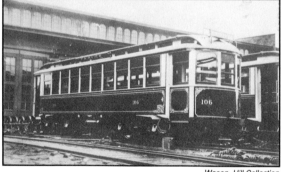

With a few exceptions, Holyoke purchased its cars from nearby Wason. Car 106, one of five 30-foot 5-inch closed cars, nears completion at the Springfield carbuilder's factory in 1905.

Pioneer western Massachusetts rail photographer Donald Shaw caught 106 on High St. by City Hall during a January 1935 snowstorm. Note the changes to the doors and the replacement of the box-type signs with roller units that had occurred over the 30 years since it had been completed, as well as the simpler paint scheme.

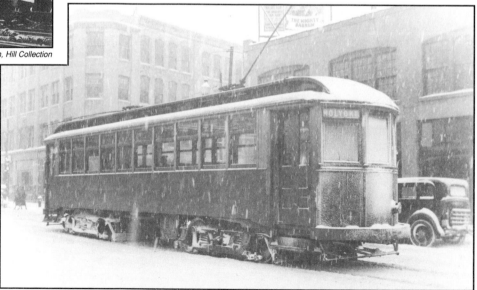

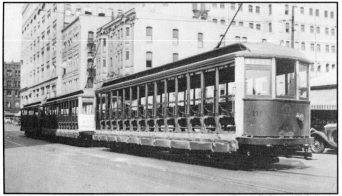

Donald E. Shaw, Hill Collection

The annual Forbes & Wallace Co. outing in June 1934 found 14-bench opens 155, 113, and 111 in Springfield. Springfield's own opens had been scrapped by this point in time.

Clark Collection

Work car W1 tows 15-bench open 151 at the Bridge St. carbarn. Note that the open has been shorn of its trolley pole, a sign that its life was nearly over.

Car 118, a 30-foot 10-inch unit, operates at High and Suffolk Sts. on the through route to Springfield in August 1931.

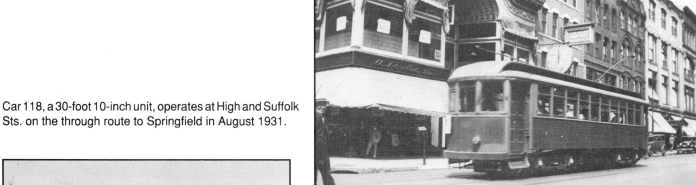

William H. Watts

Pitt Holland, Hill Collection

A 31-foot unit built by the Holyoke Street Railway, car 120 is at the end of the Fairview line in March 1935.

Charles A. Duncan

Car 134 leaves the private right-of-way after crossing the bridge at Chicopee Falls.

One of the HSR's longest lines ran from Holyoke to Sunderland through Hadley, Granby, and Amherst. In August 1931 cars 138 and 132 pass at Burnett's turnout in South Hadley while running on the Amherst service.

William H. Watts

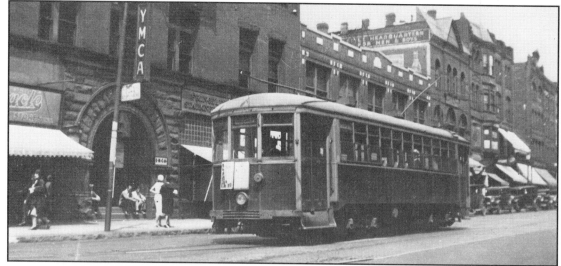

Laconia-built car 152 passes the YMCA at High and Appleton Sts. in downtown Holyoke in the summer of 1931.

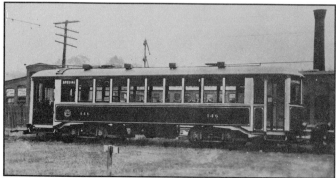

Holyoke 140-146 (even numbers only) were unique on the roster in having Westinghouse HL multiple-unit controls rather than standard type K apparatus.

The only Brill products in Holyoke built by the parent company in Philadelphia were former New York & Stamford cars. No. 158 of that lot is at the Bridge St. carbarn.

Around 1924 Holyoke acquired several cars from its Northampton partner. Former Northampton 78 at City Hall in 1935 was a 1917 Laconia product.

The newest cars on the Holyoke Street Railway were the four former Concord, Maynard & Hudson units purchased in 1923. They spent 14 years on their new owner's property, as compared with 4 in the hands of their original owner. This 1919 product of Cleveland's Kuhlman Car works, which, like Wason, was a Brill subsidiary, is at Mountain Park.

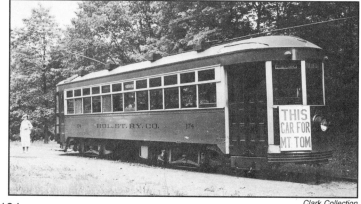

Carlson Collection

From 1897 to 1936 Mountain Park, the Holyoke Street Railway's resort area, boasted a mile-long incline railway up Mount Tom. The electrically-powered cars were counterbalanced and featured three systems of braking. The "Elizur Holyoke" leaves the Lower Station. It will meet the "Rowland Thomas" on a passing siding midway up the line.

Northampton Street Railway

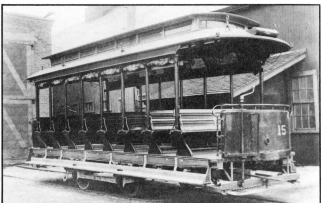

Clark Collection

Horsecar 15 of the Northampton Street Railway was of the 8-bench variety.

Clark Collection

NSR 15-bench opens 55 and 57 flank Holyoke 163 at Florence, Mass., on a special charter trip to Mount Tom.

Charles A. Duncan

In 1901 Wason delivered four 30-foot closed cars. Car 60 of that lot is at the Bay State-Florence Junction in June 1933, about six months before the end of rail service.

NSR 68, one of three 27-foot units built by Wason in 1910, operates on Pine St. in Florence after an early winter storm in November 1933.

William H. Watts

Car 62 passes through the center of the college town of Amherst in November 1933.

William H. Watts

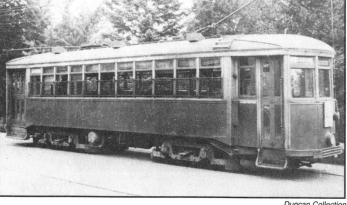

Duncan Collection

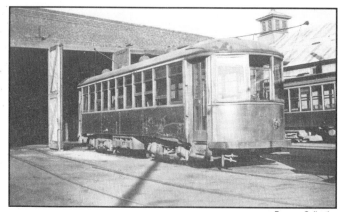

Duncan Collection

In 1917 Laconia delivered a pair of cars numbered 76 and 78 to Northampton (ABOVE). In 1924 they were transferred to Holyoke. Also transferred were 1913-vintage Wason cars 72 and 74. One of the latter pair (RIGHT) renumbered HSR 176 crosses over the Boston & Maine Railroad at Aldenville in Chicopee in August 1935. About the time of the equipment transfers to its sister company, Northampton acquired the Connecticut Valley's North Hatfield and Amherst lines, together with CV cars 116 and 118. One of the ex-CV cars (ABOVE RIGHT) leaves the carhouse as NSR 88.

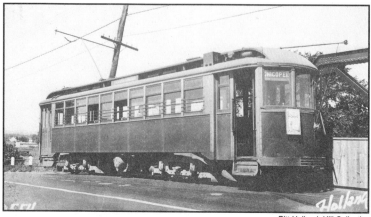

Pitt Holland, Hill Collection

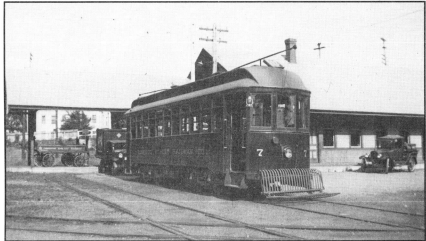

The Linwood Street Railway initiated service on January 1, 1899. Owned by Marsten Whitin of the Whitin Machine Works, the road used the tracks of the Whitin Machine Works industrial line. Car 7 is at the Whitins Station in the Linwood section of Northbridge.

William H. Watts

In May 1934 Linwood car 6 runs along the company's private right-of-way at East End, Whitinsville. The line was abandoned a few months later, on February 28, 1935.

William H. Watts

Lowell & Fitchburg Street Railway

THE LOWELL & FITCHBURG STREET RAILWAY opened on May 31, 1906, and provided a bridge between the Boston & Northern at North Chelmsford and the Fitchburg & Leominster at Ayer. It also held franchises for projected lines from Ayer to Concord and from Ayer to Nashua, N.H. The line continued in service until August 1, 1929.

Single-truck car 6 provided service on the Westford branch. The public library is in the background of this shot at Westford Center.

Rockwell Collection

Duncan Collection

Cars 8, 12, and 16 are lined up at the L&F's Ayer carhouse in November 1916. No. 16 would be sold to the People's Railway of Nanticoke, Pa., in June 1925.

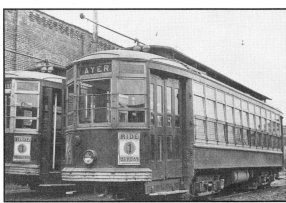

Charles A. Duncan

After July 1, 1926, all service was provided by Eastern Mass. cars and ran through to Lowell. Carrying signs for this operation is Eastern Mass. 4392 at Lowell carhouse.

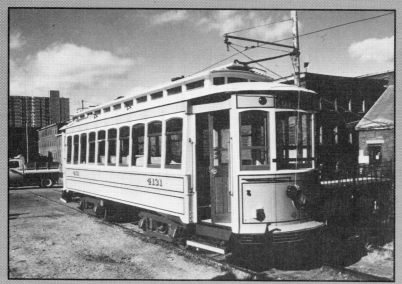

Semi-convertible 4131 is on the lead track to the Boott Mill coal pocket, which serves as the line's carbarn, on the day of its delivery to the park, November 6, 1987. A faithful replica of the Bay State 4101 series of 1912, the car has been dedicated to the memory of Theodore Santarelli de Brasch, a founder and long-time president of the Seashore Trolley Museum, who served as a technical adviser to the National Park Service during its construction.

Jim Nigzus, Jr.

THE LOWELL PARK TROLLEY originated out of the need to provide transportation for visitors between the various units of the national park site. After three summers in which a gas-electric railcar on loan from the Strasburg Railroad in Pennsylvania operated over B&M trackage, two new 15-bench opens took over in May 1984. The cars, and a closed unit acquired three years later, were based on Bay State/Eastern Mass. prototypes, and were built by Gomaco, an Iowa road paving machinery manufacturer, using mechanical and electrical equipment from Melbourne, Australia. During 1988 construction began on extensions to two of the line's three legs to serve Lowell's new Jack Kerouac Park and the Suffolk Mill complex.

Nahant & Lynn Street Railway

NAHANT

Have you ever trolleyed to Nahant?

There is no place in New England to equal it for nature's work of art.

The famous fish dinners of the "Relay House" cannot be excelled.

Good music and special attractions.

The line of cars are within ten feet of the water for two miles.

There is no other ride like it.

Cars every fifteen minutes, and when conditions require, seven and a-half minute time from Central Square, Lynn.

Nahant & Lynn Street Railway Company
LYNN, MASS.
J. E. DOZIER, Manager

Trolley Wayfinder, 1911

Duncan Collection

The Nahant & Lynn Street Railway opened on July 20, 1905, to connect Central Sq., Lynn, with the town of Nahant. Promoted principally by Bill Littlefield of the Littlefield & Moulton Box Shop, the line used Boston & Northern trackage from its Mount Vernon St. terminal to Lynn Beach. It lasted until 1930, when Eastern Mass. buses took over the entire route. Cars 19 (ABOVE), one of five McGuire-Cummings 13-bench opens purchased second-hand, and 10 (LEFT), a Brill semi-convertible bought new in 1910, wait in front of the Lynn *Daily Evening Item* Building.

Munroe Collection

138

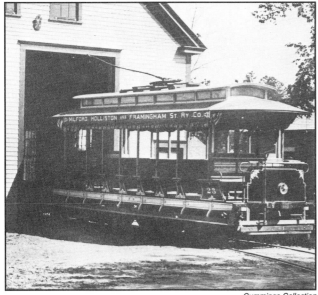

Cummings Collection

Duncan Collection

The Milford, Holliston & Framingham Street Railway opened in 1898. The Massachusetts Car Co. supplied its initial roster of fifteen 10-bench opens, including car 23, here at the Holliston carhouse.

In 1900 Jackson & Sharp constructed three 28-foot combination cars for the MF&H. On July 10, 1902, the MF&H was absorbed by the Milford & Uxbridge Street Railway, incorporated in May 1901.

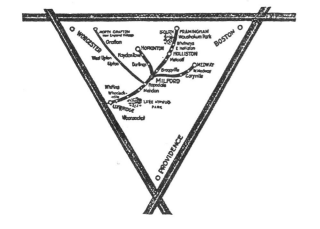

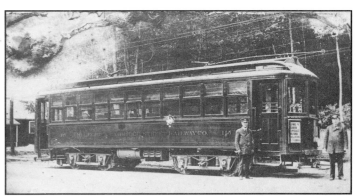

Clark Collection

M&U 115 was one of seven 30-foot units built by Wason in 1902.

Milford & Uxbridge Street Railway

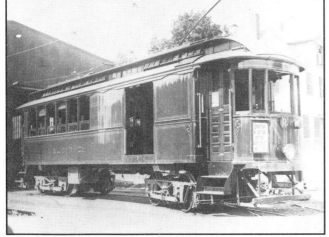

Rockwell Collection

In addition to its own lines, the Milford & Uxbridge operated the passenger service of the Grafton & Upton Railroad, and, after 1914, the lines of the Medway & Dedham Street Railway. A Jones-built 30-foot combine carries signs for service over the G&U and M&U tracks between Grafton and Milford via West Upton, Upton, and Hopedale.

The six Wason lightweights purchased in 1923 were credited with "substantial savings" in power, equipment, and track maintenance costs. They were not capable, however, of saving the line, which ran its last cars on the final day of 1928.

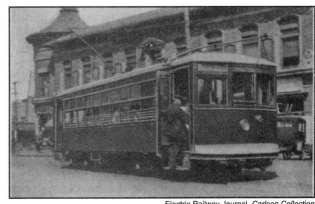

Electric Railway Journal, *Carlson Collection*

Rockwell Collection

A car of the Norfolk Southern Street Railway passes the Carpenter School on Central St., Foxborough, on its way to Mansfield on the opening day of the line, April 8, 1898. High construction costs drove the company into receivership in November of that year. It emerged two years later under Stone & Webster auspices as the Norfolk & Bristol Street Railway. It served the towns of Foxborough, Walpole, Norwood, Mansfield, and Wrentham.

Jackson & Sharp 10-bench open 22 (RIGHT) poses on East St. in Walpole in 1911. Motorman Henry Morrison is seated on the front platform, while conductor Phil Leonard stands beside the car. Leonard later became Walpole's chief of police.

Everett L. Murray, Walker Transportation Collection

Duncan Collection

In June 1906 the N&B received three 30-foot 2-inch convertible cars from Laconia. A shopman shows how the units were changed from winter to summer use in this view of car 39. When the N&B ended 1918 with a deficit, the company sought subsidies from the towns it served. Before action could be taken, the line's employees struck on August 16, 1919, for higher wages. Service never resumed, and the company's assets were sold in 1920 to satisfy creditors.

Norwood, Canton & Sharon Street Railway

INCORPORATED in March 1900, the Norwood, Canton & Sharon Street Railway opened its line from Norwood to Canton 14 months later. A joint service with the Blue Hill Street Railway, the crews simply changed hat badges as they moved from the tracks of one company to those of the other. Although not directly managed by it, the NC&S was nonetheless a part of Stone & Webster's complex of lines in southeastern Massachusetts. The

NC&S's other line opened in September 1901 and ran from Cobb's Corner in East Sharon to Lake Massapoag via Sharon and Sharon Heights. The NC&S ceased operation in March 1918, but the Cobb's Corner to Sharon Heights segment reopened as the Sharon Street Railway on August 1, 1919. Purchasing its power from the Blue Hill, its operation was ended by the same 1920 blizzard which shut down its neighboring line.

American Car Co., Rockwell Collection

Carlson Collection

NC&S 11 (RIGHT) on Day St., Sharon, is a sister to car 9 (LEFT) at the American Car Co. plant in St. Louis in July 1905.

Norton & Taunton Street Railway

Chartered in 1897, the Norton & Taunton Street Railway opened on August 27, 1898. In the following year it absorbed three other small lines, the Norton & Attleborough, the Mansfield & Norton, and the Mansfield & Easton. N&T 1 poses at Norton.

Duncan Collection

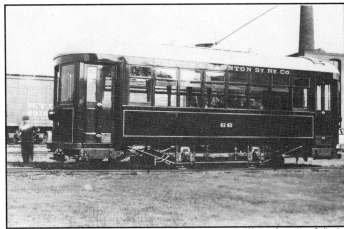

Wason, Cummings Collection

In July 1915 the N&T went into bankruptcy. Later in the year it received several new single-truck cars from Wason, including no. 66.

The Norton & Taunton was reorganized in 1917 as the Norton, Taunton & Attleborough Street Railway, coming under municipal ownership in 1920. Service was provided with Birney cars leased from the Eastern Mass. at a cost of 6 cents per car mile. Three of those cars meet at Norton. The line continued until July 22, 1928.

Clark Collection

Providence & Fall River Street Railway

OPENED IN 1901, the Providence & Fall River Street Railway served the towns of Swansea, Rehoboth, and Seekonk. Beset with the usual financial problems, it was reorganized in September 1917 as the Swansea & Seekonk. The move failed to save the property, which was abandoned on August 2, 1919.

Cars 23 and 6 (BELOW) are at the Swansea carhouse, while open 14 (RIGHT) passes under the Victory Arch on Main St. at City Hall, Fall River, in early 1919.

Duncan Collection

Duncan Collection

Horsecar 1 of the Cottage City Street Railway meets the steamer *Marthas Vineyard* at Highland Wharf on July 12, 1892. Electrifying its line in 1895, the company became the Cottage City & Edgartown Traction Co. in 1903. Five years later it was renamed the Oak Bluffs Street Railway when the island community of Cottage City changed its name to Oak Bluffs. The entry of the United States into World War I in 1917 hastened the end of service on the line, which depended exclusively on summer tourism. It was the only street railway in Massachusetts which never owned a closed car. Lettering on the trolley (LEFT) reads "Highland Wharf and Sea View Avenue."

Plymouth & Sandwich Street Railway

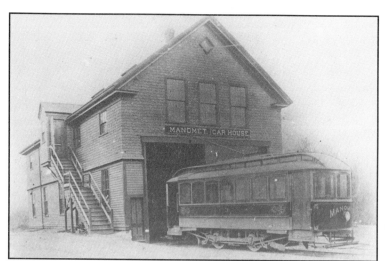

The Plymouth & Sandwich Street Railway received its charter on April 28, 1898. Running south from Plymouth to Manomet, it never achieved its ultimate destination on Cape Cod. Car 3 is pictured at the two-track wooden Manomet Car House.

For one season only the Plymouth & Sandwich operated its 11-mile line from Manomet to the Sagamore Bridge in Bourne. An unidentified 10-bench open is at Fresh Pond in South Plymouth. The P&S ceased operations in 1919.

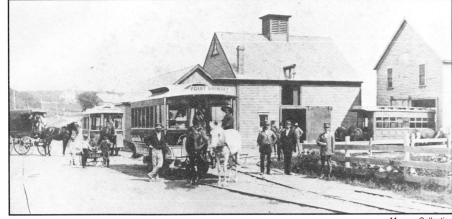

Munroe Collection

Not all horsecar lines survived into the electric era. The Winthrop Horse Railroad was one such property. Its cars operated from East Boston to Point Shirley between 1872 and 1877. This view shows cars 3 and 4 on Revere St. in front of the company's barn. The construction of what would become a part of the Boston, Revere Beach & Lynn Railroad's Winthrop Loop led to the railway's demise.

The Point Shirley Street Railway was built in 1910 to provide service over a 1.2-mile route from the Winthrop Beach railroad station to Point Shirley. The only company chartered as a street railway in Massachusetts in this century not to use overhead wires for power, its initial rolling stock consisted on three cars purchased from the Boston Elevated and converted to gasoline-electric operation by Herbert N. Ridgeway. People crowd around car 2 (ex-BERy 506) on the opening day, August 21, 1910.

Carlson Collection

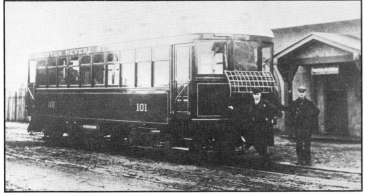

Munroe Collection

The Point Shirley came under the control of the BRB&L in late 1911. In April 1919 it received two Edison battery cars from the New York Belt Line Railroad. Only one of those units, car 101, has ever appeared in photographs. They provided service until 1928, when buses took over.

Car 3 of the Stoughton & Randolph Street Railway boards passengers at Stoughton Sq. The bankrupt line was sold to the Bristol & Norfolk Street Railway in January 1903. The B&N ran from Holbrook Depot to Randolph, Stoughton, and Easton and lasted until the late 1910s.

Carlson Collection

143

Formed on January 2, 1905, the Southeastern Electric Companies was a holding firm for the stock of the Taunton & Pawtucket Street Railway. On the same date, the Taunton & Pawtucket took over the property of the Bristol County Street Railway. That line had opened in March 1901 to connect Taunton and Pawtucket. It suffered the same problem as many other properties in the southeastern portion of the state—it ran through a sparsely-settled area and was unable to make a profit, leading to receivership.

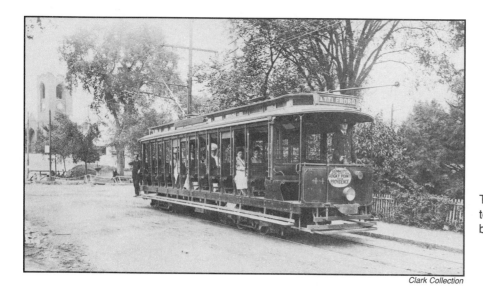

The T&P also operated a line from Attleborough to Briggs Corner, Attleborough. Car 44, piloted by motorman Walter Peckham, is on that route.

Taunton & Pawtucket Street Railway

Motorman John Fahey poses in the door of Bristol County Street Railway car 1 while conductor John Johnson leans against the side. Although the Bristol County was taken over by the Taunton & Pawtucket in 1905, it continued as a corporate entity, and the receivers, not the T&P, reported the route's statistics to the state.

The Taunton & Pawtucket ended operations on March 14, 1918. The city of Attleboro stepped in to save the 2-mile line to Briggs Corner, setting up the Attleboro & Briggs Corner Street Railway to operate it. In 1920 it purchased one Birney car from Osgood Bradley which was the line's sole piece of equipment for the remaining seven years of operation. The detrucked body of A&BC 1 rested for many years in Norton, the location where photographer Charles Duncan found it.

Warren, Brookfield & Spencer Street Railway

THE WARREN, BROOKFIELD & SPENCER STREET RAIL-WAY, inaugurated on June 25, 1896, formed part of an alternate route between Worcester and Springfield. The other portion of that line belonged to the Ware & Brookfield Street Railway, which commenced operation in December 1905 as the successor

Ware & Brookfield Street Railway

to the bankrupt Hampshire & Worcester (opened in 1901). Going into receivership in 1912, the WB&S emerged three years later as the Worcester & Warren. Like many small properties, both the Ware & Brookfield and the Worcester & Warren were hard hit by the inflation of the war years, ceasing operation in 1918.

Clark Collection

Car 12 of the Warren, Brookfield & Spencer, a product of the Massachusetts Car Co. of Ashburnham, heads for Spencer at East Brookfield. The man in uniform on the running board is Henry Clark, superintendent of the road.

Cummings Collection

A man alights from one of the Ware & Brookfield's five cars.

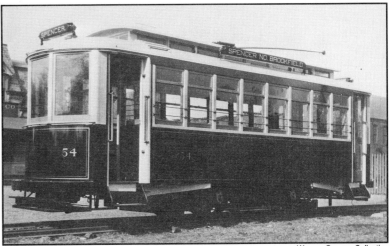

Car 54, posed at the Wason plant, was part of a three-car order purchased by the WB&S receiver. After abandonment, they were sold to the Portsmouth, Dover & York Street Railway in southern Maine.

Wason, Quance Collection

In June 1939 a three-car train of open platform coaches pauses at the Crescent Beach station of the Boston, Revere Beach & Lynn Railroad in Revere. Popularly known as the "Narrow Gauge," the electrified commuter line was within 18 months of final abandonment. Overhead-powered rail transit would return to this location in 1954 with the opening of the Revere Extension of the Metropolitan Transit Authority's East Boston Tunnel rapid transit line.

HOOSAC TUNNEL, NANTASKET BEACH
& THE NARROW GAUGE

ELECTRIFIED OPERATIONS OF STEAM RAILROADS

ALTHOUGH MASSACHUSETTS was never home to significant mileage of electrified steam railroad lines, the three major class I roads serving the state each had a segment powered by overhead wires. In addition, the commonwealth's major narrow-gauge line converted to electric operation, as did a short line freight road. (This last railroad is covered in the following chapter.)

The New Haven Railroad gained control of the Boston & Maine Railroad in the early 1900s. During this period, management took steps to end a problem which had plagued the Hoosac Tunnel ever since it opened in 1875: smoke and fumes from steam locomotives passing through the 5-mile-long "Great Bore." Seeing the success of the 11,000-volt AC electrification of the New Haven mainline west of Stamford, Ct., railroad officials decided to employ the same technology to alleviate the hazards associated with the tunnel.

Construction of electrification for the 8-mile segment from just east of the tunnel to North Adams began in November 1910. Work proceeded rapidly, and on May 18, 1911, the first train was hauled through the tunnel behind the new Baldwin-Westinghouse electric locomotives. Power for the system came from the Zylonite electric plant of another New Haven property, the Berkshire Street Railway.

The electrics were a total success, and for the first time it became possible to see light at the ends of the tunnel from its central point. The coming of diesel power during World War II, however, was to spell the end of electric operation. Since the new locomotives did not have the smoke problem of the steamers they replaced, they did not need the electric engines to take them through the tunnel. On August 23, 1946, the last motor ran through the Hoosac Tunnel. It was the earliest conversion in the United States of mainline service from electric to diesel operation.

———————

THE NEW HAVEN had earlier converted two branchline services in Massachusetts to trolley-style electric operation. Planning for the system's pioneer electric line began shortly after the acquisition of the Old Colony Railroad in 1893. On June 30, 1895, the 7-mile Nantasket Beach Branch began regular electric service. It employed 600-volt DC overhead, but extensions encompassing the route from Nantasket Junction to East Weymouth, Braintree, and Cohasset used a center third rail.

In December 1900 a second New Haven electric line started. This was the Providence, Warren & Bristol Branch, which included a leg from Warren, R.I., to Fall River. (Also in southeastern Massachusetts, the Attleborough Branch Railroad, another New Haven property, electrified after 1903, but it was operated as a part of the Interstate Consolidated Street Railway rather than as a segment of the actual New Haven system.)

Public outcry against the third rail led to the conversion of the Braintree–Cohasset line back to steam power after 1902. The Nantasket line, however, continued, despite declining traffic due to automobile competition in the 1920s, until May 1933. It outlasted the Fall River line by a little over a year.

———————

ONE OF THE MOST FONDLY-REMEMBERED operations in Massachusetts, the Boston, Revere Beach & Lynn Railroad opened its 3-foot gauge line from Line through Revere to East Boston on July 22, 1875. From East Boston, railroad-owned ferries carried commuters across Boston Harbor to their offices in the city proper. Subsequently, the railroad constructed a loop line off of the mainline to serve Winthrop.

The "Narrow Gauge" was a success from the start, and was responsible for much of the development of Revere Beach into a major recreation area. Hopes for a more efficient, and consequently more profitable, railroad led a new management in the mid-1920s to electrify the line. The first of the 60 coaches converted to multiple-unit electric cars ran on October 19, 1928, and the conversion was complete two months later.

But the Depression, followed in 1934 by the opening of the Sumner Tunnel into Boston, hit the railroad hard. In 1937 the company filed for bankruptcy, and on January 27, 1940, the line was abandoned and its assets sold to satisfy its creditors. A decade later, much of its right-of-way was used for the Revere Extension of the Metropolitan Transit Authority's East Boston Tunnel rapid transit line.

Three of the seven electric motors then owned by the Boston & Maine are seen on a passenger extra in August 1937. Lead unit 5006 was one of two acquired in 1916 to augment the original fleet due to increased traffic. In normal circumstances the electrics hauled steam locomotives and their trains through the tunnel, but this movement was a railfan special.

During the summer of 1937 three units near the point where westbound trains dropped their electric motive power at North Adams. Soon the P-4 Pacific will be the only engine on Boston to Troy, N.Y., baggage and express train no. 64.

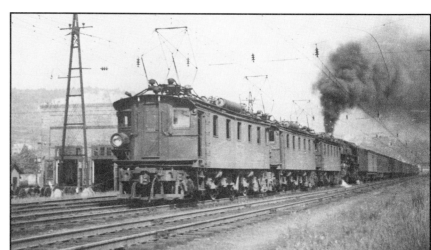

In May 1938 two motors lead a train into the east portal of Hoosac Tunnel. The motors were similar to the pioneer New Haven AC locomotives, two of which would be added to the B&M roster in 1942 to help handle heavy wartime traffic.

One of the original Jackson & Sharp open motor cars of the Nantasket Beach electrification rests between runs with trailer coach 783 at the Pemberton yard. The Pemberton House, the major resort at the tip of Hull Neck, can be seen to the left of the train. At 50 feet 4 inches, the opens were the longest cross-bench cars built in the United States.

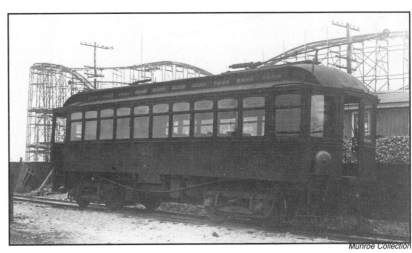

Coach 3326 was built by Bradley in 1899 for the Providence, Warren & Bristol operation, but later saw service on the Nantasket line. The location here is Paragon Park at Nantasket.

New York New Haven and Hartford RAILROAD

LOCAL TIME-TABLE.

NANTASKET BEACH BRANCH.

BETWEEN

NANTASKET JUNCTION AND PEMBERTON.

IN EFFECT APRIL 17, 1915.

Subject to Changes and Corrections Without Notice.

This Time-Table shows the times at which trains may be expected to arrive at and depart from the several stations, but their arrival or departure at the times stated is NOT GUARANTEED, nor does the Company hold itself responsible for any delay or any consequences arising therefrom.

The time of connecting lines is shown only for the convenience of the public. This Company will not be responsible for errors or changes that may occur.

C. L. BARDO,   A. B. SMITH.
GEN'L MANAGER,   GEN'L PASS'R AGT.,
NEW HAVEN, CONN.   BOSTON, MASS.

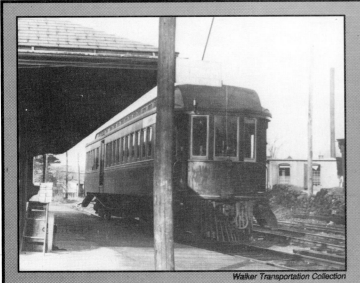

THE BOSTON & ALBANY "PING PONG"

From February 1, 1900, to April 27, 1930, Wason-built combination car 11 shuttled back and forth along the Boston & Albany's 1.2-mile Newton Lower Falls Branch. It was one of the shortest electric operations by any mainline railroad in the United States. Nicknamed the "Ping Pong" because of its short run, it is seen here at the Newton Lower Falls station. Power was furnished by the Middlesex & Boston Street Railway, and it was the imminent conversion of the last M&B lines to buses which caused the discontinuance of the electrified service.

Mason-built 2-4-4T 10 of the Boston, Revere Beach & Lynn was brand new when this picture of her with a train was taken at the Lynn terminal in 1887. Built at a cost of $10,000, it served the line until the completion of electrification in 1928.

Munroe Collection

Munroe Collection

Locomotive 19 (Alco-Manchester, 1907) heads a train on the Winthrop Loop in the summer of 1928 during the electrification of the Narrow Gauge by General Electric. The last steam-hauled train ran on December 2, 1928. While most of the steam engines were scrapped in 1929, 60 of the 95 wooden Laconia-built coaches were equipped as motor cars.

BOSTON, REVERE BEACH & LYNN R.R.

Announcing a New Rapid-transit Service

To-day, an electric train, the first of a complete electric service, has been placed in operation between Boston and Lynn. Early in November, after the electrification has been completed, the entire service will be:

FASTER—A radical reduction in running time and in time between trains; and in addition, express service for certain hours of the day.

MORE COMFORTABLE—Absence of all smoke and cinders; smooth starting and stopping; and brilliant lights for your reading at night.

SAFER—New automatic signals and air brakes.

While this electrification has progressed faster than any other of its type, and entirely without accident, nevertheless certain delays were inevitable. The Company expresses to its patrons its appreciation of their courtesy in overlooking these necessary interruptions in service.

BOSTON, REVERE BEACH & LYNN R.R.

Boston Globe, Munroe Collection

The BRB&L advertisement (ABOVE) tells the story for the picture of the inaugural multiple-unit train (LEFT) on October 19, 1928.

General Electric, Hauck Collection

In 1936 the BRB&L ferryboat *Ashburnham* (LEFT) leaves Boston for East Boston. The Custom House, Boston's first and for many years only skyscraper, can be seen to the left. Two years later, a two-car train (RIGHT) is at Winthrop Highlands station on the Winthrop Loop. The Narrow Gauge service was predominantly of the prepayment type, closer to rapid transit than steam railroad in practice.

In 1932 and 1933 the railroad purchased four 4300-class semi-convertibles from the Eastern Massachusetts Street Railway for "owl" service on the Winthrop Loop in an effort to reduce operating costs. Car 200 (ex-Eastern Mass. 4345) poses at Battery station on the loop during an October 1939 National Railway Historical Society excursion. Battery station had opened at a slightly different site in 1888 as Cherry St., being moved and renamed after the 1890 establishment of Fort Banks.

On the last day of service, January 27, 1940, a train (LEFT) enters the tunnel near the East Boston ferry terminal. On the last train for Lynn (RIGHT) souvenir-takers display their loot. Their happiness was to be short-lived, for Lynn police would be on hand to help the BRB&L reclaim its property.

An electric railway freight terminal opened on Copps Hill Wharf in Boston in 1913. The Boston Elevated's facility was shared by the Bay State and the Boston & Worcester Street Railways. In December 1917 Bay State express car 2 is at that location. The freight sheds were destroyed on January 15, 1919, when a 2.5-million gallon molasses tank on the property collapsed. Also destroyed in what writer Alton Hall Blackington called "one of the most unusual accidents ever to happen in New England" were one B&W and three Bay State freight cars and a segment of the BERy's Atlantic Ave. Elevated.

FREIGHT ALSO RODE THE TROLLEY

NON-PASSENGER SERVICE IN MASSACHUSETTS

ALTHOUGH PASSENGER SERVICE remained the mainstay of street railway lines in Massachusetts, freight and express carriage generated revenues for 20 of the state's 38 operating companies in 1916 of slightly under $1 million. Commodities handled were primarily perishables, milk, and general merchandise. In addition, several lines earned revenue by carrying mail. Although some switching of railroad cars took place, most of the business was handled by express cars or freight motors.

The small Conway Electric Street Railway in 1894 became the first line to be granted common-carrier freight rights. Two years later the Shelburne Falls & Colrain also received these rights. In both instances, freight played a major role in the history of these isolated lines in the western part of the commonwealth. Indeed, from 1907 to 1921, the last year for which breakdowns are available, the latter line's freight revenue exceeded that from passenger operation.

Not surprisingly, the major freight carrier in the state was the massive Bay State system. In 1916 it received 45 percent of the total freight revenue reported by street railways. The Bay State's predecessor, the Old Colony, had begun service in 1906 with a line from Taunton to Providence, R.I. By 1916 it served all of the major communities on its lines south of Boston. Together with the Boston & Worcester, it utilized the Copps Hill Wharf terminal of the Boston Elevated Railway in Boston's North End. (Most of the Elevated's freight income came not from its own operations but from charges for the running of Bay State and B&W cars over its tracks to reach this terminal.) While the Bay State sought and obtained rights for freight service north of Boston, it never exercised them. The successor Eastern Mass. discontinued freight operation on June 16, 1920, citing wear and tear on equipment and tracks and interruption of passenger service. The majority of the line's 44 express cars were then rebuilt for snow removal duties.

The second largest carrier, the Electric Express Co., was organized in 1907 to represent all of the New Haven Railroad's streetcar lines in Massachusetts, plus the Attleborough Branch Railroad. (The Berkshire, which had no connections with the other New Haven lines, withdrew from Electric Express at the end of 1912, but continued operating its own routes out of Pittsfield to Great Barrington, North Adams, and Bennington, Vt., until the late 1920s.) Express service between Worcester and Springfield began on January 1, 1913, two weeks after the Boston & Worcester Street Railway had started operations east of the central Massachusetts city. Until February 1, 1921, however,

shipments had to be transferred from one company's cars to the other's at Worcester.

At its height, the Electric Express, in association with the Boston & Worcester and the Rhode Island Co., provided through services from Springfield to Boston and Providence by way of Worcester. In conjunction with the Fitchburg & Leominster, it operated between Worcester and Fitchburg. After 1919 through service was also available from Springfield north to Holyoke, Northampton, and other points in the Connecticut Valley. The freight business came to an end on July 1, 1927, with the cessation of rail service between Worcester and Springfield. The Boston & Worcester continued its operations for another few months, finally abandoning them on April 14, 1928.

An interstate express route between New Bedford and Providence, R.I., via Fall River was started by the Dartmouth & Westport and the Providence & Fall River Street Railways in May 1905. This service came to an end with the closure of the Swansea & Seekonk (the successor to the P&FR) in August 1919. The Union Street Railway maintained the New Bedford–Fall River operation for another two years.

Space does not permit a detailed discussion of all freight operations. Suffice it to say that in 1916 there were four properties with freight income in excess of $50,000—Bay State ($420,149), Electric Express ($159,316), Boston & Worcester ($90,333), and Boston Elevated ($70,733). Seven others had earnings in five figures—Union ($44,163), Berkshire ($34,818), Northern Massachusetts ($18,945), Shelburne Falls & Colrain ($16,272), Holyoke ($14,491), New Bedford & Onset ($11,433), and Fitchburg & Leominster ($10,634). At the bottom of the revenue scale were the Connecticut Valley ($8,536), Brockton & Plymouth ($5,890), Conway Electric ($6,500), Massachusetts Northeastern ($2,914), and Middlesex & Boston ($2,683).

The development of reliable motor trucks, together with the general decline of the railway industry, helped speed the end of trolley freight during the 1920s. The last electric express operation in the commonwealth, however, continued until June 26, 1946, when the Grafton & Upton Railroad, which was legally classified as a steam railroad, ended operations with its former Worcester Consolidated freight motor.

Massachusetts also had a number of electrified industrial railways. These lines, serving factories and power plants, were but a minor sidelight in the story of trolley freight service in the state, and are only sampled in this chapter.

Eastern Mass. express car 8 and Boston & Worcester 513 share the rebuilt Copps Hill Wharf terminal in May 1919. A little more than a year later, on June 16, 1920, the Eastern Mass. discontinued express service. The B&W continued using the facility until April 14, 1928. Car 8 was one of the few products of the Danville Car Co. to operate in the Bay State.

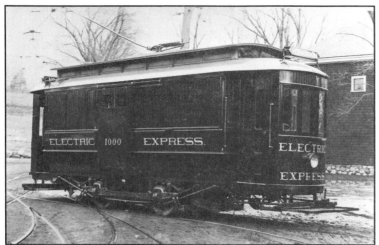

Middlesex & Boston express car 1000 served the company's sole express route, from South Framingham to Westborough via Ashland and Hopkinton.

The Fitchburg & Leominster provided joint service with the Worcester Consolidated and the Northern Massachusetts, reaching Gardner, Lunenburg, Ayer, Orange, and Worcester. Express car 2 was built in the company's shops.

Express car 304 of the Union Street Railway is on the New Bedford & Onset, its sister property, at Onset. The car was built by Jones in 1911 and sold to the Boston & Worcester Street Railway in 1923. The NB&O ran freight service between New Bedford, Wareham, and Monument Beach from 1902 to 1922.

154

The Boston Elevated's major freight operation in the 1910s was transferring molasses tank cars from Copps Hill Wharf to the Purity Distilling Co. in East Cambridge. In 1917 Universal side dump 3239 hauls Purity Distilling Co. 102 at the Albany St. yard.

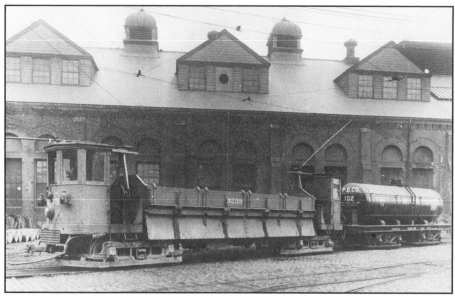

Boston Elevated Railway

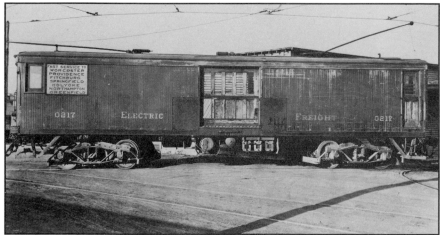

Clark Collection

The New Haven trolley freight service was handled by a separate firm, the Electric Express Co., although the cars themselves were owned by the individual railways. Worcester Consolidated 0217 was one of four express cars built for it by Bradley in 1918.

Berkshire Street Railway 0601 poses at South Lee. This express car was rebuilt in 1907 from combination passenger-baggage car 14 of the Bennington & Hoosick Valley Street Railway. It was converted to flat trailer 026 about 1912.

Cummings Collection, NHRHTA Archives

Duncan Collection

Brockton & Plymouth express car 101 was a true home-built unit, having been constructed in 1907 by B&P carpenter Wells Elliot in the back yard of his North Hanson home. The roof and other structural parts came from a former Plymouth & Kingston 8-bench open. The B&P's express route between Plymouth and Whitman ran from 1907 until 1918.

Western Massachusetts Street Railway 99 was constructed by Wason in 1905 as a double-truck nose plow. Around 1912 the unit had its plows removed and replaced by MCB-style couplers for use as a locomotive for shifting railroad boxcars. Renumbered 057 on the Springfield Street Railway roster, it survived until 1937.

Cummings Collection

Charles A. Brown

Charles A. Duncan

Surplus express cars provided work equipment for many lines. Former Springfield Street Railway freight motor 0416 (LEFT) is seen as a service car in October 1938. The Eastern Mass. converted its units into snow sweepers or plows. Sweeper E-9 (RIGHT) is at the Stoneham end of the Fellsway line in February 1939. It survived until 1948, having spent 28 years in its second role compared with 11 in its original configuration.

GRAFTON & UPTON RAILROAD

In November 1936 Grafton & Upton Railroad mail and express car 0213 meets General Electric 30-ton locomotive 8 and its train at West Upton. The G&U, which had been electrified in 1902, was a freight-only railroad, the Milford & Uxbridge Street Railway providing passenger service over its rails. Dieselized in 1946, the G&U remains in business in 1989 as a short line common carrier.

Charles A. Duncan

STREET RAILWAY POST OFFICE SERVICE

WHILE MANY STREET RAILWAYS carried mail pouches, only a few had true Railway Post Office service. The first street railway RPO in the state was on the West End, where operation commenced on May 1, 1895, on several routes covering the entire Boston system. A March 1906 timetable shows six lines radiating out from Post Office Sq. to Roxbury, Brighton, North Cambridge, Dorchester, Malden, and Somerville, with a nightly Boston Circuit RPO connecting all of these points. Service ended in the summer of 1915, when motor trucks took over.

Also in 1895, the Williamsburgh & Northampton RPO, the first interurban electric railway mail route in the country, opened. Six years later service began between Springfield and Northamp-

ton, being extended to Greenfield in 1905. The Green & Spring RPO was a joint operation by the Springfield, Holyoke, Northampton, and Connecticut Valley Street Railways and lasted until September 30, 1919.

From March 1900 to January 1910 the interstate Exeter & Amesbury RPO was operated by the Exeter, Hampton & Amesbury and the Amesbury & Hampton Street Railways.

The longest-lived RPO route in Massachusetts was the Wareham & Fall River. It commenced in March 1906 and continued until September 1927. Its closure was dictated by the abandonment of the New Bedford & Onset Street Railway, over whose rails the service ran east of New Bedford.

Wason, Clark Collection

Northampton Street Railway 38 served the Railway Post Office route from Northampton to Williamsburgh by way of Florence and Leeds. It was also used briefly on the Springfield to Northampton route in 1901.

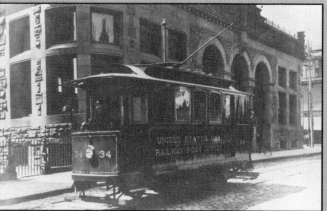

Hauck Collection

In May 1906 Union Street Railway RPO car 34 passes the New Bedford post office on William St. Preserved at the Seashore Trolley Museum, it was used in conjunction with first day of issue ceremonies for the streetcar commemorative postage stamps in October 1983.

Smithsonian Institution

Railway postal service in Boston started in 1895 with a fleet of ten cars rebuilt from horsecars. One of those units (ABOVE) sits at Post Office Sq. In 1901 the roster was supplemented by car 642 (RIGHT), here posed at Bartlett St. shops shortly after its conversion from a 25-foot passenger car.

Boston Elevated Railway

From 1918 to 1939 this 50-ton General Electric steeple cab served the United States Armory in Springfield, using Springfield Street Railway tracks between the armory's two plants. An electric meter in the cab measured power consumption in order to calculate proper reimbursement for the railway. In November 1940 locomotive A was stored at the SSR's Hooker St. yard. Shortly afterwards, it was sold to Quebec's Montreal & Southern Counties interurban, where it served as no. 325 until 1961.

C. L. Siebert, Hauck Collection

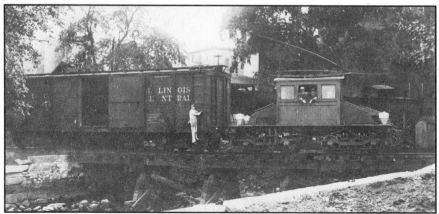

The Amesbury Industrial Railway's Baldwin-GE steeple cab hauls an Illinois Central boxcar across "dizzy bridge" in the 1930s. The line, which used power from the Mass. Northeastern, opened on September 12, 1916.

Munroe Collection

The Whitin Machine Works in Northbridge operated two industrial railways, one standard gauge, the other two-foot gauge. Standard gauge locomotive 1, built in Lynn by General Electric in 1892, was one of the earliest electric engines constructed in the United States specifically for hauling freight.

Cummings Collection

Russell F. Munroe

Rockwell Collection

The Salem Terminal Corp. switched the New England Power Co. plant at Salem. Locomotive G (LEFT) is seen out of service in 1951. The Joe Cushing Railroad (RIGHT) was an industrial line in Fitchburg. Note the large bells on the roof of two of its General Electric locomotives.

BIBLIOGRAPHY

THE FOLLOWING BIBLIOGRAPHY is necessarily selective. It omits articles in contemporary trade journals, official reports, and most pieces in the railfan press. A listing of many of these items, together with local histories that cover transit developments, can be found in Thomas R. Bullard, *Street, Interurban and Rapid Transit Railways of the United States: A Selective Historical Bibliography* (Forty Fort, Pa.: Harold E. Cox, 1984). In a few instances unpublished studies have been given when they are of value to the student of transit history.

Anderson, Edward A. *Boston's "Dallas" Cars*. Bulletin 5. Cambridge: Boston Street Railway Association, 1965.

_____. "The Lowell Park Trolley," *Rollsign*, 22 (Jan./Feb. 1985).

_____. "Lowell—Past and Present," *Rollsign*, 23 (Jan./Feb. 1986).

_____. *PCC Cars of Boston, 1937-1967*. Bulletin 6. Cambridge: Boston Street Railway Association, 1968.

Barber, Richard L. "The History of Boston's Crosstowns," *Rollsign*, 22 (May/June, July/Aug. 1985).

Becker, Philip C. *Worcester Consolidated St. Rwy. Company, 1917*. [Typescript] 1969.

_____. *Worcester Consolidated Street Railway*. [Typescript] 1965.

Borrup, Roger. "Shelburne Falls & Colrain Street Railway Company," *Transportation Bulletin*, 75 (July 1967/Dec. 1968).

_____, and Carl L. Smith. "Hyde Park Division, Bay State Street Railway," *Transportation Bulletin*, 82 (Jan./Dec. 1975).

Boston Elevated Railway Co. *Fifty Years of Unified Transportation in Metropolitan Boston*. Boston: Boston Elevated Railway, 1938.

Brown, Burton G., Jr. "The Boston Subway, 1897," NRHS *Bulletin*, 38 (No. 3, 1973).

Brown, Charles A. "The Attleboro Branch Railroad," *Shoreliner*, 12 (No. 2, 1981).

_____. "Berkshire Street Railway," *Shoreliner*, 9 (Fall 1978).

_____. "Electric Locomotives of the Whitin Machine Works," *Shoreliner*, 12 (No. 4, 1981).

_____. "The Electrification of the Nantasket Branch," *Shoreliner*, 11 (No. 4, 1980).

_____. "Milton Branch, Shawmut Branch," *Shoreliner*, 10 (No. 3, 1979).

_____. "Nantasket Branch Electrification," *Shoreliner*, 12 (No. 2, 1981).

Byron, Carl R. *A Pinprick of Light: The Troy and Greenfield Railroad and its Hoosac Tunnel*. Brattleboro, Vt.: Stephen Greene Press, 1978.

Carey, Frank P. "Boston Transit History to 1937," *Rollsign*, 11 (Jan., Feb. 1974).

Carlson, Stephen P. *All Aboard! Public Transit in Saugus*. Booklet 1. Saugus: Saugus Historical Society, 1980.

_____. "The 'Queen Mary'—Boston's First PCC Car," *Rollsign*, 24 (July/Aug. 1987).

_____, and Thomas W. Harding. *Worcester Trolleys Remembered: A Pictorial Review of the Streetcar Era in the Heart of the Commonwealth*. Worcester: Worcester Regional Transit Authority, 1985.

_____, and Fred W. Schneider, III. *PCC—The Car That Fought Back*. Special 64. Glendale, Calif.: Interurban Press, 1980.

Cheney, Frank J. "Cars Every Seven Minutes—Quincy to Boston," *Rollsign*, 21 (May/June 1984).

_____. "Eighty Six Years of the Washington Street Elevated," *Rollsign*, 24 (Mar./Apr. 1987).

_____. "Mattapan—140 Years," *Rollsign*, 24 (Jan./Feb. 1987).

_____. "The MTA and Rapid Transit," *Rollsign*, 22 (Nov./Dec. 1985).

_____. "Ninety Years at Arborway," *Rollsign*, 21 (Sept./Oct. 1984).

Chiasson, George. "East Boston Tunnel No. 4 Type Cars," *Rollsign*, 18 (July/Aug. 1981).

_____. "LRV's in Boston: The Road Back," *Rollsign*, 19 (Mar./Apr. 1982).

_____. "No. 12 Main Line El Cars," *Rollsign*, 18 (Sept./Oct. 1981).

Clarke, Bradley H. *The Boston Rapid Transit Album*. Bulletin 17. Cambridge: Boston Street Railway Association, 1981.

_____. *The Boston Transit Album*. Bulletin 14. Cambridge: Boston Street Railway Association, 1977.

_____. *Rapid Transit Boston*. Bulletin 9. Cambridge: Boston Street Railway Association, 1971.

_____. *South Shore: Quincy-Boston*. Bulletin 10. Cambridge: Boston Street Railway Association, 1972.

_____. "The Street Car Lines of Hyde Park, West Roxbury, and Roslindale, 1903-1953," *Rollsign*, 5 (Aug./Sept. 1968).

_____. *The Trackless Trolleys of Boston*. Bulletin 7. Cambridge: Boston Street Railway Association, 1970.

_____. *Trackless Trolleys of the Fitchburg & Leominster Street Railway Co.* Bulletin 11. Cambridge: Boston Street Railway Association, 1975.

_____. *Transit Boston, 1850-1970*. Bulletin 8. Cambridge: Boston Street Railway Association, 1970.

_____. "Transit Development in Belmont, 1850-1973," *Rollsign*, 10 (Aug./Sept. 1973).

_____. "Transit Development in Jamaica Plain," *Rollsign*, 11 (Aug./Sept. 1974).

Conant, Lawrence D. *New Bedford Pictorial: A Picture Roster of the Union Street Railway*. Forty Fort, Pa.: Harold E. Cox, 1980.

Cudahy, Brian J. *Change at Park Street Under: The Story of Boston's Subways*. Brattleboro, Vt.: Stephen Greene Press, 1972.

Cummings, O. R. "4-Wheel Open Cars of the Union Street Railway," *Trolleygrams*, 1-A (July 1982).

_____. "The Bay State Street Railway: 1300 and 1700 Class Semi-Convertible Cars," *Transportation Bulletin*, 50 (July 1958).

_____. "Bay State Street Railway: Trolley Freight and Express Operations," *Transportation Bulletin*, 64 (Aug./Sept. 1960).

_____. "Berkshire Street Railway," *Transportation Bulletin*, 79 (Jan./Dec. 1972).

_____. *The Blue Hill Street Railway*. Bulletin 25. Chicago: Electric Railway Historical Society, 1957.

_____. "Brockton & Plymouth Street Railway," *Transportation Bulletin*, 59 (July/Sept. 1959).

_____. "Concord, Maynard & Hudson Street Railway," *Transportation Bulletin*, 74 (Jan./June 1967).

_____. "Eastern Massachusetts Street Railway: Birney Cars," *Transportation Bulletin*, 56 (Jan./Feb. 1959).

_____. "Eastern Massachusetts Street Railway: General Description of Rolling Stock," *Transportation Bulletin*, 48 (May 1956).

Cummings, O. R. "Eastern Massachusetts Street Railway: Semi-Convertible Cars," *Transportation Bulletin*, 55 (Dec. 1958).

_____. "Eastern Massachusetts Street Railway Company: Open and Closed Cars Rebuilt or Retained," *Transportation Bulletin*, 69 (Oct. 1963/Nov. 1964).

_____. "Eastern Massachusetts Street Railway Company: Snow Fighting Equipment," *Transportation Bulletin*, 70 (Dec. 1964).

_____. "Eastern Massachusetts Street Railway Company: The 6000 and 7000 Class Cars," *Transportation Bulletin*, 71 (Jan./Mar. 1965).

_____. "Exeter, Hampton & Amesbury Street Railway," *Transportation*, 5 (1951).

_____. "Greenfield & Montague Transportation Area: A Municipal Transit Operation," *Transportation Bulletin*, 60 (Oct./Dec. 1959).

_____. *Haverhill & Amesbury Street Railway.* Warehouse Point, Ct.: Connecticut Valley Chapter, NRHS, 1948.

_____. *Massachusetts Northeastern Street Railway.* 5 vols. Forty Fort, Pa.: Harold E. Cox; Manchester, N.H.: New England Electric Railway Historical Society, 1964-67.

_____. "Massachusetts Northeastern Street Railway, 1913-1930," *Transportation*, 2 (Jan. 1948).

_____. "The Modern Car Era on the Union Street Railway," *Trolleygrams*, 2-A (Sept./Oct. 1983).

_____. "New Bedford & Onset Street Railway Predecessors—1885-1901," *Trolleygrams*, 3-A (Jan./Dec. 1985).

_____. "New Bedford's Trolley Mail Service," *Trolleygrams*, 2-A (Nov. 1983/ July 1984).

_____. "Single Truck Closed Cars of the D.&W.," *Trolleygrams*, 1-A (June 1982).

_____. *Street Cars of Boston.* 6 vols. Forty Fort, Pa.: Harold E. Cox, 1973-80.

_____. *Surface Cars of Boston, 1903-1963.* Forty Fort, Pa.: Harold E. Cox, 1963.

_____. "The Trolley Air Line: A History of the Boston & Worcester Street Railway," *Transportation*, 8 (1954).

_____. "Trolley Freight in the New Bedford Area," *Trolleygrams*, 2-A (Nov. 1983/July 1984).

_____. "The Trolley Parlor Cars of New England," *Transportation Bulletin*, 58 (May/June 1959).

_____. *Trolleys Along the Turnpike.* Bulletin 12. Cambridge: Boston Street Railway Association, 1975.

_____. *Trolleys to the Casino: Exeter, Hampton & Amesbury Street Railway.* Manchester, N.H.: New England Electric Railway Historical Society, 1969.

_____. "Union Street Railway," *Transportation Bulletin*, 85 (Jan./Dec. 1978).

_____. "Union Street Railway 4-Wheel Closed Cars," *Trolleygrams*, 1-A (May 1982).

_____. "Union Street Railway Double Truck Open Cars," *Trolleygrams*, 1-A (Aug. 1982).

_____. "Union Street Railway 'Odd Ball' Cars," *Trolleygrams*, 2-A (July/Aug. 1983).

_____. "Union Street Railway's Double Truck Suburban Cars (Incl. Dartmouth & Westport and New Bedford & Onset)," *Trolleygrams*, 2-A (May/June 1983).

_____. "Union Street Railway's 'Yellow Belly' Cars," *Trolleygrams*, 1-A (Sept. 1982).

_____, and Gerald F. Cunningham. "The Haverhill, Georgetown & Danvers Street Railway, Georgetown, Rowley & Ipswich Street Railway System, 1900-1906," *Transportation Bulletin*, 67 (Aug. 1962/Feb. 1963).

Dana, Edward. "Metropolitan Transit Authority, Boston, Mass.: Riverside Line Extension, 1959," *Transportation Bulletin*, 65 (Oct. 1960/June 1961).

DeCelle, Kenneth F. "The 'Green and Spring': Trolley RPO in the Connecticut Valley of Massachusetts," *Trolley Days in Connecticut and Up the Connecticut Valley*, 1 (July/Aug. 1983).

_____. "The Hampshire & Worcester Street Railway," *Trolley Days in Western Mass.*, 1 (Jan./Dec. 1985).

_____. "In 1895 Greenfield, Mass., Finally Got the Trolley: The Greenfield & Turners Falls Street Railway Co.," *Trolley Days in Western Mass.*, 1 (Jan./ June 1984).

DeCelle, Kenneth F. "Northampton & Amherst Street Railway Co.," *Trolley Days in Western Mass.*, 1 (July/Dec. 1984).

_____, and Philip C. Becker. "The Warren, Brookfield & Spencer Street Railway Co.," *Trolley Days in Western Mass.*, 1 (Jan./Dec. 1986).

Driscoll, Richard A. "Eastern Mass. St. Ry. Melrose-Woburn Division," *Motor Coach Age*, 36 (May 1984).

Fegley, Bruce, Jr. "Atlantic Avenue Elevated," *Rollsign*, 9 (June/July 1972).

Heinen, Roger J. *The Street Railway Post Offices of Boston.* Omaha, Nebr.: Mobile Post Office Society, 1981.

Hilton, George W., and John F. Due. *The Electric Interurban Railways in America.* Stanford, Calif.: Stanford University Press, 1960.

Humphrey, Thomas J., and Norton D. Clark. *Boston's Commuter Rail: Second Section.* Bulletin 20. Cambridge: Boston Street Railway Association, 1986.

Jenkins, Roger. *Brockton Street Railway.* [Typescript] 1982.

Johnson, Gary. "Eastern Massachusetts Street Railway Co.," *Motor Coach Age*, 34 (Aug./Sept. 1982).

Kenney, William V., ed. "Trolley Freight in Massachusetts," *The Turnout*, vol. A. (n.d.).

Lane, John J. *The Trolley Wayfinder.* Boston: New England Street Railway Club, 1911 (1972 reprint).

Mason, Edward S. *The Street Railway in Massachusetts: The Rise and Decline of an Industry.* Cambridge: Harvard University Press, 1932.

Massachusetts Bay Transportation Authority. *A Chronicle of the Boston Transit System.* [Typescript] 1981.

McGarigle, Bob. "Nantasket Beach Branch," *Transportation Bulletin*, 90 (Jan./ Dec. 1981).

McMurdo, Raymond G. "Capsule Glimpse of Worcester's Trolleys," *Rollsign*, 14 (Mar./Apr. 1977).

Mears, Sherman. *Essex Electrics.* Essex: Essex Historical Society, 1981.

Middleton, William D. *The Time of the Trolley.* Milwaukee: Kalmbach Books, 1967.

_____. *When the Steam Railroads Electrified.* Milwaukee: Kalmbach Books, 1974.

Mitchell, Walter. "Providence, Warren, Bristol," *Shoreliner*, 7 (Winter 1976).

"Norfolk & Bristol Street Railway Co.," *Transportation Bulletin*, 66 (Aug. 1961/ July 1962).

Rapid Transit Cars in Boston. Bulletin 3. Cambridge: Boston Street Railway Association, 1964.

Rapid Transit Lines in Boston. Bulletin 4. Cambridge: Boston Street Railway Association, 1965.

Schneider, Fred W., III, and Stephen P. Carlson. *PCC—From Coast to Coast.* Special 86. Glendale, Calif.: Interurban Press, 1983.

Sebree, Mac, and Paul Ward. *The Trolley Coach in North America.* Special 59. Cerritos, Calif.: Interurbans, 1974.

Shaw, Donald E. "Conway Electric Street Railway," *Transportation*, 3 (Apr./ June 1949).

_____. "The Joe Cushing Railroad," *Trolley Days in Connecticut and Up the Connecticut Valley*, 1 (May/June 1983).

_____. *Springfield Street Railway, 1870-1942.* [Typescript] 1942.

_____. "Trolley Freight in Western Massachusetts," *The Turnout*, July 1949.

_____. "The United States Armory Railroad in Springfield," *Shoreliner*, 13 (No. 1, 1982).

Stanley, Robert C. "The Main Line El," *Rollsign*, 14 (Jan./Feb., July/Aug. 1977).

_____. *Narrow Gauge: The Story of the Boston, Revere Beach & Lynn Railroad.* Bulletin 16. Cambridge: Boston Street Railway Association, 1980.

Tucker, Carleton E. "Brockton Street Railway Co.: The Beginning of the Old Colony Street Railway," *Transportation Bulletin*, 63 (May/July 1960).

_____. "Taunton Street Railway Company, Taunton Division, Old Colony Street Railway Co., and the Independent Lines Operating in Taunton, Massachusetts: The Horsecars and the Electrics," *Transportation Bulletin*, 68 (Mar./Sept. 1963).

Young, Robert H., Jr. "The Mount Tom Electric Railway," *Historical Journal of Massachusetts*, 13 (Jan. 1985).

Zeiba, George. "The Eastern Mass. Quincy-Weymouth Districts," *Motor Coach Age*, 35 (Feb. 1983).